Catholics and Protestants; What's the Difference?

A Basic Theological Analysis

Second Edition

Richard B. Ramsay

Catholics and Protestants; What's the Difference?
A Basic Theological Analysis
Second Edition

Richard B. Ramsay

ISBN: 979-8-90148-111-0
Staten House

Bible quotations are from the *New International Version*
(NIV84), unless Indicated otherwise.

CONTENTS

Dedication

I would like to dedicate this book to two Catholics that I love and respect very much, to my father-in-law and mother-in-law,

José Guillermo Pérez Flores
and
Alicia Cornejo Albornoz

I have fond memories of our conversations about the faith and our Lord Jesus Christ. Thank you for accepting me into your family, for your understanding, for your hospitality, and for your kindness.

Above all, thank you for María Angélica,
a beautiful wife, inside and out!

2007

Don Guillermo, you said you had your "bags packed" and were "waiting for the train." Angelica reminded you that the "ticket was already paid for" by Jesus. I suggested that you didn't need to pack anything at all. Now that you have gone, we miss you and look forward to being reunited with you one day in the presence of the Lord.

2011

The Author

Dr. Ramsay was a missionary in Chile for 21 years, teaching in a seminary and planting churches. There he met his wife, Angelica. They now live in Florida and they have two adult children. For the past 25 years, they have worked internationally in distance education, traveling to teach classes and producing resources for theological education and leadership training. Richard has taught for *Universidad FLET* and *Thirdmill Seminary*, and has developed many online courses.

He holds a D.Min. degree and an M.Div. from *Westminster Theological Seminary*, as well as a Th.M. from *Covenant Theological Seminary*.

Other books by the author include *The Certainty of Faith, Am I Good Enough?, Basic Greek and Exegesis, Intellectual Integrity, Transformed into the Image of Jesus, Strengthen Your Faith, Synopsis of the Bible, Putting the Pieces Together,* and *Orientation for Leaders.*

Preface

"What's the difference between Protestants and Catholics?" That's the question people often asked me during the twenty-one years I lived in Chile as a missionary. It's the main reason I am drafting this book.

Before becoming a Protestant in her university years in Chile, my wife grew up in a Catholic family, like most Latin Americans. Maria Angelica has helped me understand Catholics, and I have learned to love them and to respect them, especially her family. We also have other close friends who are committed Catholics, and I think of them as I write.

I grew up in a Protestant family in the United States. I didn't really know much about Catholics. They had their own schools, so I didn't have any Catholic friends, but my mom said they were good people. I remember watching their services and rituals on TV that seemed strange to me, with the priests in their elegant robes and head coverings, waving the smoking incense burners. Even studying the history of western civilization, the Catholic Church seemed distant and mysterious to me. When I spent a year in Germany during college and travelled to other countries, I became more aware of the importance of the Catholic presence. I was impressed with the majestic cathedrals that testified to a cultural and religious heritage of centuries. Furthermore, since I was struggling with my own faith in the Bible and key Christian doctrines, without much fellowship or support, I was glad to meet committed Catholics who at least believed in God, Jesus, and the Bible.

But I didn't really take a careful look at the differences between Catholics and Protestants until living in Chile. Over the years, I learned more about Roman Catholicism, not just about their official doctrine, but how it affected people in their daily lives. Hopefully, I developed better answers to the questions people asked.

I hesitated to publish this book for a while. I was afraid it might be misused or cause conflicts among friends and families. However, I believe it's important to clarify the differences, and I believe that we can learn to do it fairly and respectfully.

My father-in-law had a good understanding of Catholic theology, while expressing a genuine faith in Jesus Christ as his Lord and Savior. Before he passed away, he read an abbreviated version of this book (in Spanish), and found it to be fair to Catholics, which greatly encouraged me.

If you are a Protestant, hopefully this book will challenge you to understand Catholicism better. I believe we Protestants often over-simplify and misunderstand Catholic doctrine. I want to be fair to them in this book, using primarily their own *Catechism of the Catholic Church* as a source.[1] I try to put myself in their place and ask how they came to believe their doctrine. They do in fact use the Bible to support their doctrine. Their most brilliant theologians have been struggling for centuries to express their understanding of Christian teaching. I believe they deserve our time and effort to understand them better.

On the other hand, if you are a Catholic, hopefully this book will help you comprehend Protestantism. I also believe that we are sometimes misunderstood by Catholics.

Furthermore, both Protestants and Catholics may also find that they gain a deeper understanding of the Bible and of their own doctrine. Many people on both sides have not studied carefully what their own church teaches.

---

[1] *Catechism of the Catholic Church*, (New York: Doubleday, 1995).

If you are an ecumenicist, this book should make you realize that there are serious differences that we can't overlook. This is another reason I decided to write it. Some fairly recent ecumenical efforts have made me curious. *Evangelicals and Catholics Together: The Christian Mission in the Third Millennium* called for dialogue and cooperation, especially in social and moral issues of the day.[2] The document was signed by prominent church leaders from both sides, but it has also been criticized. Many agree that we can cooperate in areas where we share common goals but shouldn't pretend that the doctrinal differences are insignificant. There was also a "Joint Declaration" signed by Lutherans and Catholics regarding the doctrine of justification. It says, "Together we confess: By grace alone, in faith in Christ's saving work and not because of any merit on our part, we are accepted by God and receive the Holy Spirit, who renews our hearts while equipping and calling us to good works."[3] This sounds good, but what does it mean? Are they really in agreement about this subject that was such a decisive issue during the Reformation?

I believe that the Protestant perspective is more biblical. However, I also believe that nobody has all the truth, and that we all stand to be corrected. Furthermore, we can love each other and cooperate with each other in projects to help the needy and improve society, even though we may not always agree theologically.

Finally, remember that God is working in surprising ways in the whole world. He has been surprising us throughout history and he continues to surprise us today. I am convinced that he would have us put away our prejudices and

---

[2] Charles Colson, and Richard John Neuhaus, editors, *Evangelicals and Catholics Together; Toward a Common Mission* (Dallas, Texas: Word Publishing, 1995), p. xxii.
[3] David Van Biema, "A Half-Millenium Rift", *Time*, July 6, 1998, vol. 152, No. 1.

preconceived notions of what he will do, how he will do it, and where he will do it.

Introduction

A few years ago, my wife and I had the privilege of visiting the *Sagrada Familia* cathedral in Barcelona, Spain. It was planned by Antoni Gaudí at the end of the 19th century, and it is still under construction. I've never seen anything quite like it. I have to admit that, when I first saw it from a distance, I thought it was rather strange. But after walking around and taking a closer look, I became fascinated by it. High steeples reach toward the heavens with crosses and colorful fruit. Light is drawn into the sanctuary from above through cone shaped openings. Nature's geometry is mingled with the architecture, and Bible scenes are sculptured every place you look. I was especially moved by a figure of Jesus being tortured.

As Protestants, sometimes we only look at the Catholic Church from a distance, and it seems strange. While I am a Protestant and don't want to minimize our differences, I think we should also take a closer look and appreciate the things we have in common. That statue of Jesus represents the most important doctrine that we share: Jesus came to die for us and rose again victoriously. But there is much more. For example, both churches confess the teachings of the *Apostles' Creed*:

> I believe in God, the Father almighty, creator of heaven and earth.
> I believe in Jesus Christ, his only son, our Lord.
> He was conceived by the power of the Holy Spirit and born of the Virgin Mary.
> He suffered under Pontius Pilot, was crucified, died and was buried.
> He descended into hell.

On the third day he rose again.
He ascended into heaven and is seated at the right hand
of the Father.
He will come again to judge the living and the dead.
I believe in the Holy Spirit, the holy catholic Church, the
communion of the saints, the forgiveness of sins, the
resurrection of the body, and the life everlasting.
Amen.[4]

We should explain one of the terms used in this creed.
When the word *catholic* is used, it does not refer to the
roman institution, but to the *universal* Church, the body of
believers around the world. At the time these creeds were
written, there was only one Christian Church, and the term
catholic was used in the original sense of the word, which
means *universal*. Notice that the word is written with a small
letter and not a capital "C." Only centuries later did they
begin to use the term to distinguish the Roman Catholic
institution from other branches of Christianity.

But the purpose of quoting this creed is to show what
we have in common. We believe in the Trinity, in creation, in
the virgin birth of Jesus, in His death and resurrection, in the
forgiveness of sins, in the Second Coming, and in eternal life!
We thank God for this creed! Most of these doctrines that
the early Church discussed and defined are officially held by
all branches of the Christian Church. As I hope to show later,
our differences are not in these beliefs, but rather in our
understanding of how salvation is *applied* to us and made
effective in us.

There are three main branches of Christianity: the
Roman Catholic Church, the Eastern Orthodox Church, and

---

[4] This version of the creed is taken from the *Catechism of the Catholic Church*, pp. 56-57.

Protestantism. The first division of the Church came in 1054, when the Western Church with its base in Rome, and the Eastern Church, with its base in Constantinople, excommunicated each other mutually. A key point of disagreement was over the authority of the pope in Rome. Those from the East did not accept him as the authority over the universal Church. The second great division was the Reformation, which has as its key date the year 1517, when Martin Luther posted his "Ninety-Five Theses." This book will explain the most important differences between the Protestant branch and the Roman Catholic Church.

We do not consider Christian the cults that have departed from basic doctrines, such as the Trinity and the teachings of the Apostles' Creed cited above, or who have added other sacred writings to the Bible. The Mormons (The Church of Jesus Christ of the Latter-Day Saints) and the Jehovah's Witnesses, are the most commonly known cults.

Within each of the three branches of Christianity there are different tendencies. Roman Catholics have the Franciscan, the Jesuit, and the Augustinian orders, for example. They have the Opus Dei movement, the Schönstadt movement, Liberation Theology, the followers of Le Fevre, and other groups. Among them there are conservative theologians that hold to traditional teachings and there are liberals that depart from them. Thomas Aquinas (1225–1274) is arguably their most influential traditional theologian, and his most famous work is the *Summa Theologica*. There are also differences among Catholics from country to country. For example, there is much more emphasis on the use of images, on pilgrimages, and on the Virgin Mary in Latin America than there is in the United States.

Protestants also have different schools of theology and diverse customs. Historically, the first distinction among

Protestants was between the Lutherans and the Calvinists. The Lutheran Church became the official church in Germany, while Calvinist churches were established especially in Switzerland, Scotland, and Holland. Normally they have names that include the words "Reformed" or "Presbyterian" such as: The Christian Reformed Church, The Reformed Church of Holland, or the Presbyterian Church in America.

The reformed creeds that are best known are *The Heidelberg Catechism, The Belgic Confession, The Canons of Dordt, The Westminster Confession of Faith,* and *The Westminster Larger and Shorter Catechisms.* Early creeds of the Baptist Church were also considered reformed,[5] such as the *London Baptist Confession* of 1689.

During the sixteenth century, one of the main points of difference between the followers of Calvin and Luther was regarding the Lord's Supper and how to explain the presence of Christ in it. However, this was not the only difference between the two. Calvin put a greater emphasis in his doctrine on the sovereignty of God, on the transformation of society, and on the pedagogical use of the law of God. His major work, the *Institutes of the Christian Religion,* is one of the most systematic expressions of theology in the history of Christianity.

The Anglican Church was established in England during the sixteenth century under the leadership of Thomas Cranmer. The English wanted to become independent of Rome, but they also wanted to avoid the "extremes" of the more radical Protestants. Cranmer wrote the *Forty-Two Articles* (1553), that were later abbreviated to *Thirty Nine Articles,* still the official creed of the Anglicans. The Articles reflect the influence of reformed doctrine, but the Anglican

---

[5] *Documents of the Christian Church,* pp. 248-250.

Church kept a hierarchical ecclesiastical structure and a more formal liturgy.[6]

A third division among Protestants was between the Calvinists and the Arminians. The followers of Jacob Arminius, a Dutch theologian, disagreed especially with the Calvinist view of predestination.

A fourth group developed out of the charismatic movement. This movement began early in the twentieth century, giving rise to denominations such as the Pentecostal churches and the Assembly of God Church. These churches emphasize the person of the Holy Spirit and the extraordinary spiritual gifts. (The term "charismatic" comes from the Greek word "charisma" which means "gift".) These churches are characterized by their joyful worship services with much time dedicated to praise, and by their tireless efforts in evangelism.

Nevertheless, the greatest difference among Protestants is the distinction between "liberals" and "conservatives." These two tendencies exist within many of the Protestant groups mentioned above (as well as among Catholics). The liberals (so called by the conservatives) do not accept the Bible as infallible, and they question many of the traditional doctrines such as the virgin birth of Christ, miracles, and the literal physical resurrection of Jesus, for example. Conservatives believe that the Bible is inerrant, and we accept the historically traditional doctrines. Considering these differences, conservative Protestants are much closer to conservative Catholics than we are to liberal Protestants.

There are so many different groups and tendencies that thousands of books could not explain them! The purpose of this book is not to clarify all such differences, but rather to

---

[6] Bengt Hägglund, *History of Theology* (St. Louis, Missouri: Concordia Publishing House, 1966), pp. 292-293.

focus on the differences between the *basic traditional* beliefs of the Catholic Church and the Protestant Church.

The question is....

What are the key differences between
Protestants and Catholics?

Some differences are obvious. For example, the Roman Catholic Church maintains organizational unity with their central base in Rome, while Protestants manifest our unity in fraternal activities such as evangelistic campaigns, conferences, and interdenominational organizations. The ecclesiastical government of the Catholic Church is very hierarchical, while the majority of Protestant churches have some kind of democratic representative system. (The Anglicans are an exception, maintaining a hierarchy.) Protestants permit our pastors to marry, while Catholics ask their priests to remain celibate. Liturgies also differ in obvious ways. In general, the Catholic service is normally more solemn and more formal, while the Protestant service is normally less formal. Catholics practice confession before a priest, while Protestants confess directly to God. There is also a difference in the Bibles used by each church. The Catholic Bible includes the "Apocryphal" books, while the Protestant Bibles do not.

But many of these differences are secondary. In this book, we will focus on what I consider fundamental doctrinal differences. The key Protestant doctrines that differ from Catholicism can be summarized in three phrases: 1. Faith Alone (*Sola Fide*), 2. The Bible Alone (*Sola Scriptura*), and 3. Jesus Alone (*Solo Christo*).

1) "Justification by faith alone" was one of the fundamental doctrines of the Reformation. Although

"Protestant" doctrines were being taught much before his time, it was Martin Luther that marked the beginning of the Reformation with his "Ninety-Five Theses" nailed to the Wittenburg door in 1517. He objected to indulgences and the authority of the pope, but justification by faith was at the heart of his theology.

2) For Catholics, the Bible is not their only source of divine revelation. They also believe that God has preserved other truths through oral Tradition, and that this truth is communicated to us through the authorities of the Catholic Church.

3) For Catholics, in one sense, Jesus is our only mediator for salvation. However, in another sense, the saints and especially the Virgin Mary are also mediators, because they intercede for us and cooperate in our salvation.

For the official Catholic view, the new *Catechism of the Catholic Church* is cited mostly in this book. This impressive volume carries the weight of approval of the Catholic authorities and is reinforced by citing official historical documents. It is both official and up to date. For the historical Protestant view, the *Westminster Confession of Faith* and the *Westminster Larger and Shorter Catechisms* are used. Although not all Catholics agree with everything in the *Catechism*, and not all Protestants agree with everything in the Westminster standards, I believe these documents represent the *traditional* positions *on the main issues discussed in this book*.

1. Salvation; the Catholic View

The following anecdote from a popular Italian novel represents many people's religious experience, among both Catholics and Protestants:

> In the entrance to the school, the sisters had built a large manger scene which remained standing all year long. There was Jesus in the stable with his father, his mother, an ox and a little donkey, and all around there were mountains and cliffs made of cardboard and rocks, where only a flock of little sheep lived. Every one of them represented a student, and depending on her conduct each day, was moved closer or farther away from Jesus. Every morning, before going to class, we would pass by the manger, and they made us look to see our position. On the other side of the stable there was a very steep cliff, and that's where the bad girls were put, with two legs suspended over the edge. From six years of age until ten, I lived conditioned by the position of my little sheep. I don't need to tell you that I hardly ever moved from the edge of the cliff. [7]

We tend to think that the distance between us and God depends directly on our conduct. So the key question is, how can I become right with God? How good do I have to be? How can I be accepted by God and be at peace with God? How can I be saved?

---

[7] Translated by the author from the Spanish version, *Donde el corazón te lleve* [Where your heart leads you] Susana Tamara (Santiago, Chile: Editorial Atlántida, 1995), pp. 66-67.

We'll look at how each church answers these questions. First, Catholics agree with us that our salvation is made available only because of God's grace. The Catholic *Catechism*[8] says:

> 1998 This vocation to eternal life is supernatural. It depends entirely on God's gratuitous initiative, for he alone can reveal and give himself....

> 1999 The grace of Christ is the gratuitous gift that God makes to us of his own life, infused by the Holy Spirit into our soul to heal it of sin and to sanctify it....

Both Protestants and Catholics point to the work of Christ as the *basis* of our salvation. Man is a sinner and deserves eternal condemnation, but Jesus came to live a perfect life and to die in our place. He took the punishment that we deserved. In these crucial points, both churches agree.

But the difference becomes apparent when we ask another question: How do we *receive* the salvation that Jesus purchased? We basically agree on how God *purchased* salvation for us, but not on how God *applies* this salvation to us.

Protestants believe we receive salvation by faith alone in Jesus Christ. We emphasize the direct work of the Holy Spirit in our hearts. By contrast, Catholics teach that, in addition to faith in Jesus, receiving salvation also depends on the sacraments, especially baptism and the Eucharist, plus the merits earned by man in cooperation with the grace of God. They emphasize the fact that the Church is the channel

---

[8] Quotes from the *Catechism* will usually be identified by the number of the section, without adding a separate footnote. This way they can also be found in any version.

for saving grace. The Catholic position is not as simple as many Protestants believe; it is not exactly *faith + works = salvation*.

This topic is the most important of all; it gets to the heart of the gospel. At first, the differences may seem very subtle, but they are actually profound.

Strangely enough, the document, *Evangelicals and Catholics Together*, does not include justification by faith among the differences that need to be discussed. Even more confusing, the document states that Evangelical Protestants and Catholics "affirm together that we are justified by grace through faith because of Christ."[9] But just what do Catholics mean when they affirm this? What do they mean by "justification," and by "faith?" Notice also that it does not say we are justified through faith *alone*.

We hope to clarify their doctrine in this chapter, and then explain the Protestant teaching in the following chapter. Again, the important question is, how does a person *receive* the saving grace of God?

I often like to ask the "Kennedy Questions" from *Evangelism Explosion:*[10]

If you were to die today, do you think you would go to heaven?

If you were to die and go before God, and he asked you why you think you could have eternal life, what would you answer?

---

[9] Colson and Neuhaus, *Evangelicals and Catholics Together*, p. xviii.
[10] James D. Kennedy, *Evangelism Explosion*, (Chicago: Tyndale House Publishers, 1977).

Many Catholics I have talked to think that it would be arrogant and presumptuous to believe they are going to heaven. Those that do think they would go to heaven often base their confidence on the fact that they have tried to live a good life or that they have suffered a lot.

How would you answer these questions?

Let's see if your answer changes by the time you finish reading this book. These questions tend to reveal what or whom you are trusting for your salvation.

At times, Catholic teaching about salvation and eternal life seems ambiguous or contradictory. It may be because they use theological terms in a different way than Protestants. It may also be because their doctrine of *Tradition* means that they accept teachings over many centuries as official doctrine, even though they may sometimes seem contradictory.

The problem of sin

First, before speaking of salvation, we should explain why we need to be saved. According to both Catholic and Protestant doctrine, "all men are implicated in Adam's sin" (*Catechism* 402, Romans 5:12, 19), "deprived of original holiness" (417). This is called "original sin" (417).

Historically, there have been different views about the extension and gravity of the effects of the Fall, as well as the nature of fallen man's freedom and ability to seek God and obey Him. The *Catechism* expresses the consequences of the Fall in one section as a "death of the soul," but in another section as "not totally corrupted," and as "wounded."

403 ...He [Adam] has transmitted to us a sin with which we are all born afflicted, a sin which is the *"death of the soul"*.[11]

405 ..Original sin...is a deprivation of original holiness and justice, but human nature has *not been totally corrupted*: *it is wounded* in the natural powers proper to it, subject to ignorance, suffering and the dominion of death, and inclined to sin..."

For the purpose our discussion in this chapter, it's sufficient to highlight our agreement that all people are under condemnation (402, Romans 5:18), in need of salvation. The original harmony has been destroyed in all dimensions (400) and all of man's history has been "the story of dour combat with the powers of evil" (409).

Initiation

There are two stages in the process of salvation, according to the Catholic view: "initiation" and "collaboration," or "initiation" and the "continued struggle."

First, a person (usually a child) receives the initial grace of God in the sacrament of baptism. Notice all the benefits of this sacrament:

1213 Holy Baptism is the *basis of the whole Christian life*, the *gateway to life in the Spirit* (*vitae spiritualis ianua*), and the door which gives access to the other sacraments. Through Baptism we are *freed from sin and*

---

[11] Most *italics* in these texts and all other quotes from the *Catechism*, the Bible, the Protestant documents, or from any other text, are mine, and not were not underlined in the original.

reborn as sons of God; we become members of Christ, are *incorporated into the Church* and made sharers in her mission: "Baptism is the *sacrament of regeneration through water in the word.*"

1263 By Baptism *all sins are forgiven, original sin and all personal sins,* as well as all punishment for sin. In those who have been reborn *nothing remains that would impede their entry into the Kingdom of God,* neither Adam's sin, nor personal sin, nor the consequences of sin, the gravest of which is separation from God.

Many vital things happen upon being baptized: 1) Sin is forgiven. This includes original sin inherited from Adam, as well as personal sins. Nothing remains that would keep the person from entering the kingdom of God. 2) The person is born again. This is called "baptismal regeneration." The statement, *Evangelicals and Catholics Together,* points out that among the differences between Catholics and Evangelicals is "Baptism as a sacrament of regeneration or testimony to regeneration."[12] The Catholic view is that baptism results in regeneration, but Evangelicals don't agree. 3) The person becomes a member of the Church, the Body of Christ. 4) He or she receives grace, which is "infused" by the Holy Spirit. Obviously, this sacrament is fundamental for Catholics. It is the beginning of their Christian life. The *Catechism* calls baptism the "first conversion."[13] It also employs the term "justification" to explain the results of baptism.[14]

---

[12] Colson and Neuhaus, *Evangelicals and Catholics Together,* p. xxi.
[13] See section 1427.
[14] See section 1992.

Protestants should be careful to avoid confusion when we read the word "justification." For Catholics, it includes both forgiveness of sin and freedom from the power of sin. In other words, their "justification" includes both *justification* and *sanctification,* as Protestants understand the terms.

> 1989 *Justification* is not only the remission of sins, but *also the sanctification* and renewal of the interior man.[15]

Afterwards, when the baptized person reaches the "age of reason," he or she participates in the *confirmation* and receives the *Eucharist*. These two additional sacraments form part of the "initiation," because they prepare the person to live a new life in Christ.

When Protestants read about the benefits of baptism for Catholics, we might ask, "Wouldn't the baptized person already be saved then?" To us it seems that, if his sins are forgiven in baptism, he has already received eternal life. The answer is, according to the Catholic view, in baptism he receives new life but can also later fall from the state of grace. According to the Catholic scheme, he still has the weakness of the sinful nature ("concupiscence"), and he can lose his state of purity that he received with the sacraments of initiation.[16]

Baptism covers original sin and personal sins committed before baptism, but not sins committed after baptism. Neither does it take away the natural sinful tendency. In other words, baptism does not guarantee eternal life.

---

[15] See also section 1990: "Justification detaches a man from sin which contradicts the love of God, and purifies his heart of sin. Justification follows upon God's merciful initiative of offering forgiveness. It reconciles man with God. It frees from the enslavement to sin, and it heals."

[16] See sections 1420 and 1426 of the *Catechism*.

405 ... Baptism, by imparting the life of Christ's grace, erases original sin and turns a man back towards God, but the consequences for nature, weakened and inclined to evil, persist in man and summon him to spiritual battle.

It's as if the person were a glass that has been filled with pure water at baptism. But when the person sins, the water becomes contaminated and must be purified again. The advantage now is that, after initiation, the person has the Holy Spirit and grace to gain merits. This takes us to the second stage of salvation.

Collaboration

The baptized person now begins the stage of struggle. He "collaborates" with God to obtain eternal life and other blessings, by earning merits and by making use of the other sacraments such as the Eucharist and Penance. This stage of purification is also called a "second conversion."

1428 ...This *second conversion* is an uninterrupted task for the whole Church who, "clasping sinners to her bosom, [is] at once holy and always in need of *purification*, [and] follows constantly the path of penance and renewal."...

1429 ...St. Ambrose says of the *two conversions* that, in the Church, "there are water and tears: the water of Baptism and the tears of repentance."

This process is especially important if he has fallen from the state of "baptismal grace" by committing a "grave" (or "mortal") sin.[17] If a person has fallen from grace and dies without forgiveness, he will go to hell.

> 1033 ...To die in mortal sin without repenting and accepting God's merciful love means remaining *separated from him for ever* by our own free choice. This state of definitive self-exclusion from communion with God and the blessed is called "hell."[18]

A "grave" sin, or "mortal" sin, is a more serious sin, especially related to breaking the Ten Commandments. It must also be committed "with full knowledge and deliberated consent" to be classified as "grave."[19]

From the moment in which the person is baptized (and "justified"), he begins this collaboration. Now his righteousness is obtained by *cooperation* with God. Since his ability to "cooperate" was graciously given to him in his baptism, they consider God to be the first cause of man's righteousness. But man's good works are also meritorious and essential to obtain salvation.

> 1993 Justification establishes cooperation between God's grace and man's freedom.

It is true that Catholicism teaches that salvation is based fundamentally on the grace (gratuitous help) of God. In the strict sense of the word, man doesn't merit anything.

---

[17] The terms seems to be synonymous, but not all Catholic theologians consider the terms exactly the same.

[18] See also 1446 "Christ instituted the sacrament of Penance for all sinful members of his Church: above all for those who, since Baptism, have fallen into grave sin, and have thus lost their baptismal grace and wounded ecclesial communion."

[19] See sections 1854-1859 of the *Catechism*.

2007 With regard to God, there is no strict right to any merit on the part of man.

Nevertheless, man has something to contribute during the stage of collaboration. In the sacraments of initiation, the person receives a new capacity to cooperate with the grace of God in the spiritual struggle. He has received this capacity by grace, but then the person himself can freely decide how he uses the capacity.

2008 The *merit of man* before God in the Christian life arises from the fact that God has freely chosen to associate man with the work of his grace. The fatherly action of God is first on his own initiative, and then follows *man's free acting* through his *collaboration*, so that *the merit of good works is to be attributed in the first place to the grace of God, then to the faithful.*

They go so far as to say that *not only daily blessings, but also eternal life depends on man's good behavior.*

2010 ...Moved by the Holy Spirit and by charity, *we can then merit* for ourselves and for others *the graces needed for our sanctification*, for the increase of grace and charity, *and for the attainment of eternal life.* Even *temporal goods* like health and friendship can be *merited* in accordance with God's wisdom.[20]

An essential part of a person's collaboration is to make use of the sacraments. The *Eucharist* is especially important

---

[20] See also section 2027.

to receive spiritual strength. It works redemption and transformation.

> 1068 For it is in the liturgy, especially in the divine sacrifice of the Eucharist, that *"the work of our redemption is accomplished...."*[21]

The sacrament of *Confession,* or *Penance*, which will be studied in greater detail in a subsequent chapter, is also a key to spiritual growth. It brings forgiveness for sins committed after baptism.[22]

What about faith? What place does it have in the Catholic view of salvation? Catholics teach that faith in Jesus is necessary for salvation.

> 161 Believing in Jesus Christ and in the One who sent him for our salvation is necessary for obtaining that salvation.

But faith is not the *only thing* necessary for salvation. It is faith *plus baptism*, faith *plus the sacraments*, faith *plus good works.*

Furthermore, when they speak of "faith," they emphasize its *corporal* aspect, or its *ecclesial* aspect. Since the Church is the body of Christ, the deposit of faith, it becomes the channel through which an individual "believes." In other words, when someone becomes a member of the Church, he shares the faith of the body as a whole.

---

[21] See also sections 1069 and 1074.
[22] See section 1422.

168 It is the Church that believes first, and so bears, nourishes, and sustains my faith.

169 Salvation comes from God alone; but because *we receive the life of faith through the Church*, she is our mother.

181 *Believing"* *is an ecclesial act.* The Church's faith precedes, *engenders*, supports, and *nourishes* our faith. The Church is the mother of all believers. *"No one can have God as Father who does not have the Church as Mother.*

This explains the importance of the sacraments. While Protestants tend to emphasize the individual believer and his personal faith, Catholics emphasize the Church and its faith as a body. The Church is their "mother" that gives birth to their faith, feeds it and takes care of it. Thus, when a person is baptized and received into the Church, he or she becomes part of the body of believers and participates in this corporate faith, leading to salvation. The sacraments then continue to be the vital connection with God's grace as it is channeled to the body. Catholics have designated this age the "sacramental economy."

1076 ...In this age of the Church, Christ now lives and acts in and with his Church, in a new way appropriate to this new age. *He acts through the sacraments* in what the common Tradition of the East and the West calls *"the sacramental economy";* this is the communication (or "dispensation") of the fruits of Christ's Paschal mystery in the celebration of the Church's "sacramental" liturgy.

Conclusion

In summary, Catholics bind up saving grace with the sacraments and with human merits. For Catholics, a person first receives initial grace in baptism. Then he or she cooperates with God to do works of righteousness, while the sacraments supply him with grace to continue this process of "justification."

The Church is the channel to receive grace, and the Church has control over how that grace is dispensed. It's as if God poured out a bucket-full of grace into the Church, and the Church in turn pours it out to its members.

At the risk of over-simplifying, the Catholic teaching about how we receive saving grace could be summed up, not by the phrase, "faith + works = salvation," but rather by the phrase, "baptism + other sacraments + faith + merits = salvation." Keep in mind that baptism produces regeneration and the forgiveness of sins. Remember also that their collaboration stage produces "justification," which includes what Protestants call sanctification.

CATHOLIC VIEW OF RECEIVING SALVATION

These elements all work together and are interdependent. A person receives faith through the sacraments, and his faith leads him to continue participating in the sacraments. The sacraments give him grace to do meritorious works, and one aspect of the works is to partake of the sacraments.

We can't understand the Catholic position until we see the importance of the sacraments and the Catholic Church as an institution. The authorities control the dispensation of grace through the sacraments. This is why a Catholic depends so much on the church and the clergy.

Questions for Review and Discussion:

1. What is the basis of our salvation, according to both Protestants and Catholics?
2. How would you answer the "Kennedy questions" about eternal life?
3. Explain the Catholic view of salvation. What is the place of sacraments in their view of salvation? Of faith? Of merits?
4. What is the meaning of baptism for the Catholic church? What benefits does it bring?
5. How does the Catholic church understand justification?
6. How do they understand saving faith?
7. What do you think of the story of the sheep and the manger? Do you sometimes identify with the sheep that is far from Jesus? How can you get closer to him? Do you think being close to Jesus depends fundamentally on your own conduct?
8. Do you sometimes ask yourself, "*Have I been good enough to be saved?*" Do you think we can know for sure that we are saved?

2. Faith Alone; The Protestant View of Salvation

John 6:28,29
Then they asked him, "What must we do to do the works God requires?" Jesus answered, "The work of God is this: to believe in the one he has sent."

There is a moving scene in the movie *The Mission*, in which Robert de Niro interprets the role of Mendoza, a slave trader of people from the Guarani tribe (from the area of the Iguazú falls) during the time of the Spanish colonization. To do penance, he had to climb a steep cliff with a rope tied to a net full of heavy objects. When he could no longer continue, a group of Guaranis came down to meet him carrying knives. He is sure that they are going to kill him but instead, they cut the rope and free him. The weighty objects go tumbling down over the rocks. This apparently symbolizes forgiveness to Mendoza, and he breaks down crying.

As I understand it, the penance exercise required of Mendoza represents human effort to obtain forgiveness, and the cutting of the rope by the Guaranis represents God's free forgiveness. It graphically illustrates the fact that we are all sinners, incapable of satisfying the justice of God or gaining our own salvation by merits, but Christ has gained it for us.

Not all people who consider themselves Protestants have a clear understanding of the Protestant view of salvation. Some may feel like Mendoza climbing the cliff, unsure of their eternal life because they think it somehow depends on their own good works. They may hold to some kind of "balancing scales" view of salvation. Others know they are saved by faith, but they think it's up to them to makes themselves better Christians after accepting Christ's forgiveness. I myself grew up in a Protestant church, but I lived a very legalistic spiritual life during my youth. I pictured God behind the two tablets of the Ten Commandments, watching me to see if I committed a sin. My Christian life was basically just trying to be good. It may not be the fault of our churches or our pastors; these notions seem to come to us naturally.

Historically, however, Protestant doctrine has been clear about salvation by faith alone. We have insisted that the only thing that we need to receive eternal life is *faith in Jesus Christ.* The sacraments proclaim the gospel with tangible and visible elements to help us believe and grow in our faith, but they don't accomplish forgiveness and salvation in and of themselves. Furthermore, we believe that good works are *consequences* of our salvation, not the *cause* of it. And just like we can't earn eternal life, we can't make ourselves good by our own efforts. Looking at how this works in the life of an individual, the steps in receiving salvation are the following, according to the Protestant view:

Regeneration

First, a person's heart must be renewed. We are all born as sinners, and our heart is so deeply affected by sin that we will not seek God in and of ourselves. Thus, God takes the initiative, sending His Spirit to revive us from spiritual death. We are "born again." This change enables us to understand the gospel and believe.

Regeneration does not depend on any sacrament or any human act. It is the free work of the Holy Spirit, done how and when he wishes. It is mysterious and invisible to the human eye. Jesus spoke of this experience with Nicodemus.

John 3:3-8

In reply Jesus declared, "I tell you the truth, *no one can see the kingdom of God unless he is born agai*n."

"How can a man be born when he is old?" Nicodemus asked. "Surely he cannot enter a *second time into his mother's womb to be born*!"

Jesus answered, "I tell you the truth, no one can enter the kingdom of God *unless he is born of water and the Spirit. Flesh gives birth to flesh, but the Spirit gives birth to spirit.* You should not be surprised at my saying, 'You must be born again.' The wind blows wherever it pleases. You hear its sound, but you cannot tell where it comes from or where it is going. So it is with everyone born of the Spirit."

There are various interpretations of this passage. Catholics agree that a person needs to be regenerated to be saved, but they believe that the complete phrase "born of water and the Spirit" refers to one experience of being born again through the sacrament of baptism (1215).

I would argue that to be born of water is one experience and to be born of the Spirit is another, that Jesus is making a *distinction* between *physical birth* and *spiritual birth* (*regeneration*). Notice first that Nicodemos asks if being "born again" means returning to the mother's womb to be born again physically (v.4), and Jesus answers him in that context. This suggests that Jesus is talking about two experiences, the first being the physical birth from the mother's womb. Secondly, notice the parallelism between verses five and six. As in many passages of the Bible, especially because of the influence of Hebrew parallelism, the second phrase explains the first, using different words. In this case, the need to be "born of water and the spirit" is parallel with the phrase, "flesh gives birth to flesh, but the Spirit gives birth to spirit." That is, to be "born of water" is another way of saying "born of the flesh" and to be born of the Spirit refers to spiritual regeneration.

But why does Jesus speak of *water*? Water is sometimes a symbol of life in the Bible (e.g., Revelation 21:6 and 22:17) and it is something absolutely necessary to remain alive. However, since his statement follows immediately after Nicodemus' reference to the mother's womb, I am inclined to think He is referring to the circumstances surrounding the physical birth of a baby. Some argue that there is no evidence that water was commonly associated with birth at that time, but it's easy to think of ways in which it instinctively would be: a) A baby is cushioned by liquid in the mother's womb (something the mother senses during the pregnancy). b) Then the leaking of that liquid (amniotic fluid) is a sign that the baby will soon be born. In our culture, we often say "her water broke." c) Finally, the baby is wet when born.

The important point for understanding the Protestant view of regeneration is that it is necessary for salvation and it is a mysterious work of the Holy Spirit, invisible, like the wind. Just as a baby does not decide to be born or take the initiative in the birth process, neither does a person decide to be born again spiritually or take the initiative in obtaining his or her salvation.

I like to ask people if they *decided* they were *going to believe* in Jesus, then some time after making the decision they actually believed, or if they *realized* at some point that they *already believed*. I have yet to hear someone say they decided to believe first, then later took the step of believing.

This shows how regeneration works. It's something the Spirit does in us, not something we control.

Repentance, Faith, and Justification

Repentance and Faith (Conversion)

The regenerated person hears the gospel and, moved by the Holy Spirit, responds with repentance and faith. This means turning from a sinful life, asking forgiveness, and following Jesus. We also call this combination of responses a "conversion." (For Protestants there is only one "conversion.") This experience may be immediately after regeneration or it may be much later. He could not believe if it were not for the supernatural work of the Holy Spirit in his heart.

Justification

Upon believing, God immediately declares him free of guilt and transfers to his legal account the righteousness of Jesus Christ. This is "justification." God treats him "just as if" he had never sinned. It is more than forgiveness, because the account is not left blank, but with the positive righteousness of Christ. It's as if he had a huge *debt* with the bank of millions of dollars, then God not only paid the debt, but also left millions of dollars to his *credit* in the account.

Remember that there is a difference between the Catholic concept and the Protestant concept of justification. Protestants define justification as a divine verdict that leaves man free from guilt and provides him with the righteousness of Jesus in his favor. We do not see it as a combination of forgiveness and interior renewal, as Catholics understand it. We do not include sanctification under the same concept as justification, but rather we consider it a distinct aspect of salvation. First comes justification, which establishes the person's *legal* status, and then comes sanctification, which is a process of *personal growth*.

The *Westminster Shorter Catechism*, question #3, says:

> What is justification?
> Justification is an *act of God's free grace*, wherein he pardoneth all our sins, and accepteth us as righteous in his sight only for the righteousness of Christ *imputed to us,* and *received by faith alone.*[23]

The *Westminster Confession* says:

> Those whom God effectually calleth, He also freely justifieth: *not by infusing righteousness* into them, but by pardoning their sins, and *by accounting and accepting their persons as righteous;* not for any thing wrought in them, or done by them, but for Christ's sake alone; nor by imputing faith itself, the act of believing, or any other evangelical obedience to them, as their righteousness; but *by imputing the obedience and satisfaction of Christ unto them*, they receiving and resting on Him and His righteousness *by faith; which faith they have not of themselves, it is the gift of God.* (ch. 11, paragraph 1)

The term "impute" means attributing to one person's account what belongs to another. When we believe in Jesus,

---

[23] Version published by the Committee for Christian Education and Publications of the Presbyterian Church in America, 1983, *The Confession of Faith of the Presbyterian Church in America, Together with the Larger Catechism and the Shorter Catechism with the Scripture Proofs*.

his righteousness is imputed to our account. Notice that faith is not considered a merit. Faith is a gift from God. It is a channel to receive salvation.

Eternal Life is Promised and Free.

In the moment he believes, the person *already has obtained eternal life.* Furthermore, once acquitted, God will never condemn him. This is why Protestants insist on "salvation by faith alone." It is a free gift, not earned by man's efforts or accomplished by receiving a sacrament, and it begins the moment he believes.

John 5:24

I tell you the truth, whoever hears my word and believes him who sent me has eternal life and will not be condemned; *he has crossed over from death to life.*

Romans 4:1-5

What then shall we say that Abraham, our forefather, discovered in this matter? *If, in fact, Abraham was justified by works, he had something to boast about* -- but not before God. What does the Scripture say? "Abraham believed God, and it was credited to him as righteousness."

Now when a man works, his wages are not credited to him as a gift, but as an obligation. However, to the man who does not work but trusts God who justifies the wicked, *his faith is credited as righteousness.*

Ephesians 2:8-9

For it is by grace you have been saved, through faith -- and this not from yourselves, it is the gift of God -- not by works, so that no one can boast.

Notice the reasoning: Since it is a free gift, *nobody can boast*. Can you imagine a heaven where everyone is comparing notes on how they got there, bragging about their good deeds! It could never be! The only attitude imaginable in heaven is one of gratitude to God for saving us!

Not By Works

We can't be saved by keeping the commandments. The law is like a *sign* pointing to Jesus. Let's imagine that we want to go to the moon, and the only way to get there is by spaceship. Let's say there is a sign pointing to the spaceship saying, "This way to the moon. You can't fly on your own! You must board this spaceship." This is similar to our spiritual situation. We want to go to heaven, and the only way to get there is by faith in Jesus Christ. The law would be like a sign pointing to Jesus, saying, "This way to eternal life. You are a sinner and therefore cannot get there on your own. You must believe in Jesus to be saved."[24] Now consider this: To try to be saved by good works would be like sitting on top of the sign and trying to ride it to the moon!

> Romans 3:19-24, 28
>
> Now we know that whatever the law says, it says to those who are under the law, so that every mouth may be silenced and the whole world held accountable to God. Therefore *no one will be declared righteous in his sight by observing the law*; rather, through the law we become conscious of sin.
>
> But now a righteousness from God, apart from law, has been made known, to which the Law and the

---

[24] Sign illustration adapted from *La Vida de Pablo* [The Life of Paul] (Viña del Mar, Chile: SEAN Internacional, Edición Experimental, 1983), p. 28-29.

Prophets testify. This righteousness from God comes *through faith in Jesus Christ* to all who believe. There is no difference, for all have sinned and fall short of the glory of God, and are *justified freely by his grace* through the redemption that came by Christ Jesus. *...For we maintain that a man is justified by faith apart from observing the law.*

Galatians 3:10-11
All who rely on observing the law are under a curse, for it is written: "Cursed is everyone who does not continue to do everything written in the Book of the Law." Clearly *no one is justified before God by the law*, because, "The righteous will live by faith."

Salvation by works cannot be combined with salvation by faith. You have to choose one or the other, because salvation by works is a direct contradiction to salvation by grace. Grace is undeserved favor. If salvation comes through faith *and merit,* it is no longer grace. If someone pays a single dollar for a car, it is no longer a gift, but a purchase.

Romans 11:6
And if by grace, then it is no longer by works; if it were, grace would no longer be grace.

The fatal error of the Jews as a nation (not all individuals) was to think they were saved by being Jews and by keeping the law. Many thought that circumcision, the sign of being a Jew, guaranteed their salvation.

Romans 9:31-32
> But Israel, who *pursued a law of righteousness*, has not attained it. Why not? Because they pursued it not by faith but as if it were by works. They stumbled over the "stumbling stone."

But Paul explains that a true Jew is one who has faith.

Romans 2:28-29
> A man is not a Jew if he is only one outwardly, nor is circumcision merely outward and physical. No, a man is a Jew if he is one inwardly; and circumcision is circumcision of the heart, by the Spirit, not by the written code. Such a man's praise is not from men, but from God.

Galatians 3:7
> Understand, then, that those who believe are children of Abraham.

Paul couldn't make it more clear! He insists that trying to be saved by good works only leads to condemnation. Why? Because it is the proud counterpart of trusting in God.

The thief on the cross could not have been baptized, nor did he have time to study theology. He didn't have the opportunity to make amends for his sins. He simply expressed repentance and faith in Jesus, asking for salvation. And Jesus declared that he was saved (Luke 23:43)!

How About the Sacraments?
For Protestants, the sacraments function much like the written Word, the Bible. When we read the Bible, the Holy Spirit uses the words to lead us to faith. The words are not

just any words, but they are incredibly special words chosen by God himself. However, it is not the act of reading the Bible that saves us, but the fact that we *believe* in the gospel. In the same way, baptism proclaims the promises of the gospel, using visible symbols. The water represents cleansing from sin and the outpouring of the Holy Spirit. But it's not the act of being baptized that saves us; it's the fact that we believe the promises represented in the sacrament.

The example of Abraham, which becomes a paradigm in the rest of Scripture, shows that faith is the key to salvation. In Romans chapter four, Paul asks if Abraham was justified *before* or *after* being circumcised. His answer is that righteousness was credited to him *before*, explaining that circumcision was a "seal of the righteousness that he had by faith *while he was still uncircumcised*." (Romans 4:10–11) Why is this detail important? Because it proves that salvation is by faith, not by receiving a sacrament or by any human merit. The sacrament represents the fact that a person *already* belongs to the people of God; it doesn't *make* a person belong.

Sanctification

The question that someone might ask at this point is, "If you are saved by faith alone, what is to keep you from living any sinful way you please?"

Saving Faith Results in Sanctification.

Our answer is found in the doctrine of *sanctification*. What is sanctification? Basically, it's spiritual growth. While justification defines our *legal* relationship with God, sanctification describes our *personal relationship*, our *daily walk* with him. They are both aspects of salvation, and they both come by faith.

While these two *concepts* are distinct, the *experiences* are *inseparable* in the life of the Christian. That is, nobody is justified without also being sanctified. Neither can anyone be sanctified without first being justified. True faith produces a change in our life. If there is no change, there is no faith; if there is no faith, there will be no change. As Protestants often say, "we are saved *by faith alone*, but *not by a faith which is alone*." The *Westminster Confession* explains:

> Faith, thus receiving and resting on Christ and His righteousness, is the alone instrument of justification: *yet is it not alone in the person justified*, but is ever accompanied with all other saving graces, and is no dead faith, but worketh by love. (Chapter 11, section 2)

In chapter six of Romans, Paul himself anticipates the difficult question about moral passivity, in response to his bold teaching on justification by faith found in the first five chapters. (By the way, if we have the same question after reading chapters one to five of Romans, it means that we understood him correctly!) His answer is that he cannot conceive of a person really believing, and then living freely in sin.

Romans 6:1-2
> What shall we say, then? Shall we go on sinning so that grace may increase? By no means! We died to sin; how can we live in it any longer?

Augustine said, "Love and do as thou wilt."[25] At first, this sounds terribly wrong. However, after analyzing it somewhat, it makes sense; it just needs to be explained properly. I think he meant that if we are really loving God and loving our neighbor, we will want to do what is right.

The point is that a person who really believes in Jesus has become a *new person*. The Holy Spirit has given him new desires and a new power over sin. Not only has he been freed from the *guilt* of sin (justification), but he has also been freed from the *power* of sin (sanctification).

> Romans 6:14
> For sin shall not be your master….

> Romans 6:18
> You have been set free from sin and have become slaves to righteousness.

Of course, the believer still struggles with sin, as Paul explains in Romans 7. But he is no longer *dominated* by it. The Christian is like a country that has changed rulers. Our new King is Jesus Christ, but the terrorists are still active. We have been healed of a cancerous disease, but there are lingering side effects.

By Faith From First to Last

How can we win the victory over sin? Only by faith in Christ! Not only is justification by faith; sanctification is also by faith. Every aspect of the Christian life is by faith. Paul

---

[25] < Philip Schaff: NPNF1-07. St. Augustine: Homilies on the Gospel of John; Homilies on the First Epistle of John; Soliloquies - Christian Classics Ethereal Library (ccel.org)> (06/01/2021)

introduces his letter to the Romans with a sweeping statement:

Romans 1:17

For in the gospel a righteousness from God is revealed, a righteousness that is *by faith from first to last,* just as it is written: "The righteous will live by faith."

Notice that the gospel message is that: 1) righteousness comes from God, and 2) it is by faith *from first to last*. Our life is like a bridge held up by four columns of the grace of God. We walk the bridge, trusting those columns, from one end to the other.

This verse says it all! It is a clear introduction to the whole letter of Romans. The first five chapters explain justification, and the rest of the letter explains sanctification. Both are by faith!

Paul also makes the same point in Galatians. False teachers had come to Galatia, confusing the new believers about salvation by faith. These teachers were insisting that they be circumcised and keep the law of Moses. In this case, Paul insisted that they should not comply, since that would be to deny the cross of Christ. We are saved by faith, not by keeping the law.

Then he argues that we began by the Spirit and should continue by the Spirit. To seek our own sanctification by our own efforts would be foolish.

Galatians 3:1-3

You foolish Galatians! Who has bewitched you? Before your very eyes Jesus Christ was clearly portrayed as crucified. I would like to learn just one thing from you: Did you receive the Spirit by observing the law, or by believing what you heard? Are you so foolish? *After beginning with the Spirit, are you now trying to attain your goal by human effort?*

We are like an electric train that is constantly connected to a cable. We depend moment by moment on the Lord directly. That is, we are in continual need of his energizing power over sin. Faith means leaning on him continually. It means we derive our spiritual strength from Jesus, just as a branch gets its life from the vine (John 15).

Catholics Have Condemned This View.

We agree with Catholics that salvation depends on the grace of God and that a person must be born again and believe in Jesus. We also agree that a Christian should strive to please God and keep his commandments. But we don't agree on the role of human effort in achieving that obedience, or on the role of the Church and the sacraments in the salvation process.

Often Catholic literature can be confusing to us Protestants. However, keeping in mind that they use the term "justification" to include what Protestants call sanctification, it's important note that the Catholic Church has *condemned* the doctrine of justification by faith alone. This is clear in the canons of the *Council of Trent*.

CANON IX.-If any one saith, that *by faith alone* the impious is justified; in such wise as to mean, that nothing else is required to *co-operate* in order to the *obtaining the grace of Justification*, and that it is not in any way necessary, that he be prepared and disposed by the *movement of his own will*; let him be anathema.

CANON XII.-If any one saith, that justifying faith is *nothing else but confidence in the divine mercy* which remits sins for Christ's sake; or, that this confidence alone is that whereby we are justified; let him be anathema.[26]

The Council insists that good works are not only the fruit of justification, but also a "cause" of the "increase" of it.

CANON XXIV.-If any one saith, that the justice received is not preserved and also increased before God through *good works*; but that the said works are merely the fruits and signs of Justification obtained, but not a cause of the increase thereof; let him be anathema.[27]

As we explained in the previous chapter, according to the Catholic view, man becomes responsible to "collaborate" with the grace of God in the second stage of salvation. One author on the *Catholic Answers* website explains that obedience is a "necessary instrument through which grace flows". This seems contradictory; if obedience is necessary to receive grace, then it's no longer grace. He adds that "there is nothing anyone can do before they enter into Christ that can justify them. But once a person enters into Christ... it's a whole new ballgame." He quotes James 2:24 and concludes, "...Are we justified by faith? Certainly! By faith alone? No way! It's *both* faith *and* works, according to Scripture."[28]

---

[26] Session 6, January 13, 1547. *http://history.hanover.edu/texts/trent/trentall.html*
[27] Session 6, January 13, 1547. *http://history.hanover.edu/texts/trent/trentall.html*
[28] Tim Staples, "Are Good Works Necessary for Salvation?"<https://www.catholic.com/magazine/online-edition/are-good-works-necessary-for-salvation>

Remember that the sacraments are also necessary in the collaboration stage of the Catholic scheme.

> 1074. ...It is in the sacraments, especially in the Eucharist, that Christ Jesus works in fullness for the transformation of men

As I see it, in the Catholic scheme, instead of being like an electric train connected to a cable, Christians are more like cars with gas tanks that repeatedly run low on gas and need to be filled again by means of the sacraments. Furthermore, following the same analogy, according to the Catholic scheme, the car can run out of gas or make a wrong turn and get lost. For Protestants, the train will always stay on the tracks.

Let me clarify again that I am talking about the official doctrine of the Church. Thankfully, salvation doesn't depend on which Church we belong to. Neither does it depend on being able to explain all the doctrines correctly. By God's grace, salvation depends only on having personal faith in Jesus.

No More Sacrifices and Ceremonies
During the Old Testament, Jewish believers related to God through a sophisticated ceremonial system. They had to go to the temple to approach God, and they depended on the priests to be their mediators. Only the high priest could pass through the curtain to enter the inner sanctuary, the Holiest of Holies, and he could only do this once a year (Exodus 26:33, Leviticus 16). However, when Jesus died, the curtain in the temple was torn miraculously, from top to bottom (Mark 15:38), symbolizing the opening for all believers to draw near to God directly.

Hebrews 10:19–22

Therefore, brothers, since we have confidence to enter the holy places by the blood of Jesus, by the new and living way that he opened for us *through the curtain,* that is, through his flesh, and since we have a great priest over the house of God, let us draw near with a true heart in full assurance of faith, with our hearts sprinkled clean from an evil conscience and our bodies washed with pure water.

Protestants want to emphasize this direct connection with God.

Conclusion

To sum up in a simple way the Protestant view of how we receive salvation, it is "regeneration + faith = salvation." Remember that true faith includes repentance and that salvation includes both justification and sanctification.

PROTESTANT VIEW OF RECEIVING SALVATION

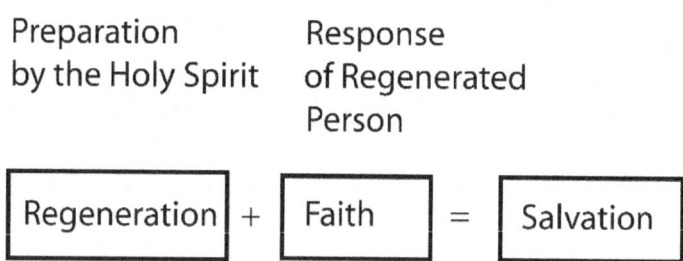

Preparation by the Holy Spirit

Response of Regenerated Person

| Regeneration | + | Faith | = | Salvation |

We could add other aspects of salvation to make the explanation more complete. For example, the Holy Spirit "calls" a person, causing him to hear the gospel and urging him to respond. Also, once a person is justified, he or she is "adopted" as God's child. Furthermore, salvation includes the final stage of "glorification," when we are made morally like Christ.

Romans 8:29-30
For those God foreknew he also predestined to be conformed to the likeness of his Son, that he might be the firstborn among many brothers. And those he predestined, he also called; those he called, he also justified; those he justified, he also glorified.

Let's sum up the differences we have seen so far:

a. For Protestants, regeneration is a direct, invisible work of the Holy Spirit. For Catholics, it is a result of the Spirit working through baptism.

b. For Protestants, justification is by faith alone and it means being declared righteous. For Catholics, it is by faith plus works plus the sacraments, and it includes sanctification as well as forgiveness.

c. For Protestants, upon believing in Christ and being justified, a person already has eternal life and will not lose it. For Catholics, a person receives eternal life in baptism, but can fall from grace.

d. Protestants emphasize our direct relationship with God in the process of sanctification. Catholics emphasize the sacraments and consider them necessary for sanctification.

Another way of illustrating the difference between the Catholic and Protestant views of salvation is to think of the difference between scuba divers and deep-sea divers. A scuba diver takes a tank of oxygen with him, whereas a deep-sea diver is directly connected with a hose that provides him with oxygen.

The Catholic view is similar to the scuba diver model. God is like the big ship that carries all the equipment and provides oxygen tanks for the divers. The Church is like a smaller boat with diving experts (the clergy), which is let down from the big ship onto the surface of the water, along with divers and oxygen tanks. Then the diving experts help the divers put on their oxygen tanks and help them get into the water. If the divers need more oxygen, they must go back up to the smaller boat and get another tank. This symbolizes the fact that, in the Catholic perspective, God turns over the management of grace to the Church and its authorities, and the Church expects the individual to collaborate with them. The Church and the clergy control the sacraments, and the individual controls his own use of the sacraments and his own gaining of merits.

In contrast, the Protestant view is more like the deep-sea diver model. In this case, the divers continually depend directly on the big ship for their supply of oxygen, which is provided through the hose. This symbolizes the fact that God supplies us directly with his grace. Nobody else in-between manages the grace. The smaller boat (the Church) is still there to help, but the diver doesn't depend on the experts in the same way they do in the Catholic scheme.

Questions for Review and Discussion

1. What is the meaning of regeneration for Protestants?

2. What is the meaning of "being born of water and the Spirit" in John 3?

3. What is the Protestant understanding of justification?

4. What is the Protestant understanding of sanctification?

5. Explain the illustration of the spaceship and the sign.

6. What is the role of baptism in salvation, according to Protestants?

7. What is the Protestant understanding of saving faith?

8. What is the means of sanctification?

9. What does Romans 1:17 teach us about justification and sanctification?

10. Explain the illustration of the electric train as opposed to a car that runs on gasoline.

11. Explain the illustration of the boats, the scuba diver and the deep-sea diver.

3. Clarifying Some Doubts

It would be dishonest to pretend that there are no biblical texts that are difficult to explain according to the Protestant viewpoint. In this chapter, we hope to clarify doubts that arise from some of these passages.

James 2 and Justification

One of the most difficult passages for Protestants to explain in regard to justification by faith alone is chapter two of *James*. It first appears to be a contradiction to Paul's teaching in Romans and Galatians. However, if we analyze it properly, we can see that there is no contradiction. Both authors wrote as they were inspired by the Holy Spirit, and are expounding the same doctrine, just from different angles, and with a slight change in the use of vocabulary. Let's take a closer look at James. The problem is especially evident in translations such as the *King James Version*, the *New American Standard*, or the *English Standard Version*. (The *New International Version* presents a problem only in verse 24.) Here is the ESV translation of verses 18-26:

> James 2:18-26
> [18] But someone will say, "You have faith and I have works." Show me your faith apart from your works, and I will show you my faith by my works. [19] You believe that God is one; you do well. Even the demons believe—and shudder! [20] Do you want to be shown, you foolish person, that faith apart from works is useless? [21] Was not Abraham our father *justified by works* when he offered up his son Isaac on the altar? [22] You see that

faith was active along with his works, and faith was completed by his works; [23] and the Scripture was fulfilled that says, "Abraham believed God, and it was counted to him as righteousness"—and he was called a friend of God. [24] You see that a person is *justified by works* and not by faith alone. [25] And in the same way was not also Rahab the prostitute *justified by works* when she received the messengers and sent them out by another way? [26] For as the body apart from the spirit is dead, so also faith apart from works is dead.

How can we understand this passage? Does it teach salvation by faith *plus works*?

1. First, notice that James quotes the same passage in Genesis that Paul quotes in Romans 4, "Abraham believed God, and it was credited to him as righteousness." It's clear that he doesn't intend to contradict Paul or to argue against the concept of justification by faith.

2. Many scholars believe that James wrote his letter after Paul wrote Galatians and Romans. Even if that is not the case, the teachings about salvation by faith must have circulated widely. It would make sense that James was correcting a possible misunderstanding of the gospel of grace. Apparently, some people were saying they had "faith," but their deeds showed that they were not true disciples of Christ.

3. James is distinguishing between false faith and real faith. False faith is dead, and it does not produce fruit. True faith is living, and it produces positive change. False faith is merely intellectual, like the faith of the demons. The demons know that there is only one God, but it doesn't change their lives.

4. The illustration in verses 14-17 about helping a brother in need is just that, an illustration. It should not be misunderstood to mean that we are saved by helping people who are suffering. Rather, James is explaining that to say you have faith without deeds is like this ironic story: If someone is hungry and has no clothes, it doesn't help him much to say, "I wish you well, keep warm and well fed!" That is, to have a supposedly loving attitude toward this person doesn't feed him and clothe him! Even more, and this is James' point, the very fact that the person only wishes him well verbally is clear *evidence* that he didn't even have a sincere *desire* to help him. The test of whether he really wishes him well is in the way he treats him. If he helps him, we know he had a good attitude. If he doesn't help him, then we know that his words were empty and insincere.

5. This helps us understand the problem of faith and good works. The good works become evidence of true faith. If they don't exist, the profession of faith becomes empty words. But if they do exist, this doesn't mean the good deeds are the meritorious basis of salvation, but it does show that his faith is sincere.

6. Now a point about the word "justify" in verses 21, 24, and 25. The root Greek word in all three verses is δικαιόω (dikaióo). The problem disappears when we realize that James is using the word in a way that is different from the way Paul normally uses it. It shouldn't surprise us, since biblical words are used in a wide variety of ways by different authors. There are several definitions of this Greek word:

1) show justice, do justice to someone
2) justify, vindicate, treat as just
3) be acquitted, pronounced and treated as righteous

4) make free or pure

5) be proved to be right [29]

Paul almost always uses the word in the third sense in Romans and Galatians. He refers to our legal standing in Christ. When God justifies us, he gives a verdict of "not guilty," in fact he declares us "righteous." However, Paul himself also uses the word in the fifth sense in Romans 3:4, when he speaks of God being "justified."

Romans 3:4

...Let God be true, and every man a liar. As it is written, "So that you may be *proved right* when you speak and prevail when you judge." (NIV84)

The Greek word translated *proved right* here in the NIV translation is δικαιόω (dikaióo). (The ESV translates the phrase as, "that you may be justified in your words".) Obviously, in this case, the term is not related to forgiveness or being legally declared innocent by a judge. God doesn't need forgiveness, and nobody is his judge. Rather, it means that God's righteousness is *proved*, or it is *made evident*.

I believe James also uses the word in this fifth sense in chapter two. He is saying that we are *shown* to be personally righteousness by our deeds. The NIV84 translates the word as "considered righteous" in both verse 21 and verse 25. In my judgment, we should also use this phrase or another similar phrase, such as "proved righteous" or "shown to be righteous" to translate the same Greek word δικαιόω (dikaióo) in all three verses, 21, 24 and 25, of the chapter.

---

[29] Arndt and Gingrich, *A Greek-English Lexicon of the New Testament and Other Early Christian Literature* (Chicago: University of Chicago Press, 1957), p.196

James is *not* saying that we merit God's forgiveness and eternal life by our good deeds. He is simply saying if you really have true faith, your righteousness will also be manifest in your life. Sanctification is *evidence* of true faith.

Matthew 25 and the Final Judgment

There is a similar problem with passages that talk of the final judgment, such as Matthew 25:31-46. It speaks of the judgment, when the Son of Man will separate the sheep from the goats. The sheep represent those who fed the hungry, showed hospitality to the stranger, gave clothes to the needy and visited people in prison. He tells them, "Come, you who are blessed by my Father; take your inheritance, the kingdom prepared for you since the creation of the world." The goats represent those who didn't help the needy. He tells them, "Depart from me, you who are cursed, into the eternal fire prepared for the devil and his angels!"

This is sobering! It makes you think, doesn't it? How does this fit our Protestant understanding of salvation by faith alone? Is Jesus teaching here that the determining factor will be our good deeds?

No! The explanation is not so complicated. Jesus is really teaching that the *evidence* of true faith will be the fruit of a changed life. It's the same point as James 2. John 15 will help us understand this better.

John 15; The Divine Illustration

The best way to put all these thoughts together is to look at a divine illustration that Jesus himself taught. It's found in John 15:

John 15:1-8

I am the true vine, and my Father is the gardener. He cuts off every branch in me that bears no fruit, while every branch that does bear fruit he prunes so that it will be even more fruitful. You are already clean because of the word I have spoken to you. Remain in me, and I will remain in you. No branch can bear fruit by itself; it must remain in the vine. Neither can you bear fruit unless you remain in me.

I am the vine; you are the branches. If a man remains in me and I in him, he will bear much fruit; apart from me you can do nothing. If anyone does not remain in me, he is like a branch that is thrown away and withers; such branches are picked up, thrown into the fire and burned. If you remain in me and my words remain in you, ask whatever you wish, and it will be given you. This is to my Father's glory, that you bear much fruit, showing yourselves to be my disciples.

This explains it all! Think about it! First, Jesus gives us the analogy: he says he is the vine and we are the branches. Then he tells us how to bear fruit: by "remaining in him." In fact, he makes the point stronger: we *cannot* bear fruit without him. Finally, he warns that he who does not remain in him will be thrown into the fire and burned.

If we relate this to the whole question of faith, works, salvation, and final judgment, it all becomes clear. We are all born as sinners. We are like a branch disconnected from the vine. Then we are told that if we do not bear fruit, we will be condemned. So what can we do?

Can you imagine a loose branch trying to bear grapes to avoid being cast into the fire? For all its effort to push and squeeze, it can't! So what can it do? There is only one way of salvation, to be grafted into the vine! How can we be grafted into the vine? By faith!

Once it becomes part of the vine, the life of the vine is transmitted to the branch, carrying water and minerals, and the branch bears fruit. This is an analogy of faith. By faith we are engrafted into the vine and can bear fruit.

How do we know if a branch is really engrafted? By the grapes! In the life of a Christian, the fruit is evidence of true faith. This is why Jesus can look at a person's good deeds on judgment day to see if there was true faith. The good deeds are not the *cause* of his salvation, but the *evidence* of his faith.

The fatal mistake is to turn these things around. Some people think that they can be saved by producing good works. But this is just like a loose branch trying to produce grapes. They can't do it! They need to first put their faith in Christ, ask him for forgiveness, turn their hearts and lives over to him, and ask him to generate the good works in them. The *Westminster Confession of Faith* says:

> We cannot by our best works merit pardon of sin, or eternal life at the hand of God, by reason of the great disproportion that is between them and the glory to come; and the infinite distance that is between us and God,... (Chapter 16, section 5)

Furthermore, when we consider the inward motivation, any "good deed" that is not the fruit of faith is not pleasing to God.

Hebrews 11:6a
And without faith it is impossible to please God....

But the more important point is that when a person becomes a Christian, his life is changed. A person should be compared, not with others, but with his own previous life. If there is no positive change, there is no evidence of faith.

Think about another illustration, an adaptation of Jesus' analogy. Let's suppose that all of us were born as orange trees, and that the only trees that could be saved are apple trees. On judgment day, God will look at the fruit to see what kind of tree we are. If we have apples, he will let us enter heaven. If we have oranges, we will be separated from him. What can we do? Start producing apples to make him think that we are apple trees? No, we can't! The only hope is to be transformed miraculously into real apple trees so that the fruit is genuine. This can only happen by faith in Jesus. He gives us new life so that we can bear genuine fruit.

Finally, one more illustration. Think about a light bulb. What makes it give out light? Is it the light bulb itself that causes light? No, it's the electricity. The light bulb is an instrument, but the electricity is the power. However, if the filament is burned out or broken, the light bulb will not produce light. Think of how this is an analogy of the Christian. We don't cause good deeds; the Holy Spirit does. However, if we do not have faith, there will be no good deeds. Thus the lack of a changed life indicates a lack of true faith.

The Covenant Concept

Another concept which runs through all of Scripture is also helpful in avoiding a libertine reaction to salvation by faith. It is the concept of the *covenant*. God entered into a covenant with Noah, with Abraham, with Moses, and with David, for example. His relationship with Israel was often expressed in terms of a pact. God promised to be with them, to be their God, to protect them and bless them. But he expected them to keep their part of the covenant as well, honoring him and obeying him. Circumcision was the sign of the covenant in the Old Testament, signifying the family's agreement to keep their part. The book of Deuteronomy itself is written in the form of a covenant, with the typical promises, blessings, demands and curses. In fact, the whole Bible is really a covenant document, with God's promise of salvation and his expectations of us as his people. We could give a long historical study of all the manifestations and stages of God's covenant relationship with his people, but that is not the purpose here.

The main point here is that being saved means entering a covenant with God. This includes accepting his promises, but it also includes committing our lives to him. God says, "I will be your Lord and your Savior if you trust me and agree to live as my disciple." The believer says, "Thank you for sending Jesus to die for me, for offering to be my Lord and my Savior! I accept your covenant and agree to live as your disciple!"

This should not lead us to think that our salvation depends on how well we keep our side of the covenant. If it did, nobody would be saved! Rather, it is in the very moment that we *accept the covenant* that we are *already* saved. What is the key factor that leads us to accept the covenant? Faith!

Acts 2:38 and Baptism

In addition to the passages that might give the impression that our good works contribute to our salvation, there are other passages that might give the impression that baptism is necessary for our salvation.

For example, in Acts 2:38, Peter says "repent and be baptized...*for* the forgiveness of your sins." Some people take this to mean that the sacrament itself produces forgiveness, or even that you must be baptized to be saved. However, this would contradict many other key passages in the New Testament that teach salvation by grace through faith alone (Romans 1:16-17, Romans 3:28, Ephesians 2:8-10, for example).

The word in Acts 2:38 translated "for" is εἰς ("eis") in Greek, which can mean "into," "in," "unto," "to," "towards," "for," "on," or "among." It helps to see that the same Greek word "eis" is used in a similar context in Romans 6:4, "We were therefore buried with him through baptism *into* death,..." Obviously, this verse doesn't mean that baptism produces death! I would argue that in both Acts 2:38 and Romans 6:4, the phrase refers to what baptism *represents*. Baptism is "for" forgiveness in the sense that it represents forgiveness, and it is "for" death in the sense that it represents our spiritual death (and resurrection) with Christ.

E4's Greek Lexicon says the following:

> "For" (as used in Ac 2:38 "for the forgiveness...") could have two meanings. If you saw a poster saying, "Jesse James wanted for robbery," "for" could mean Jesse is wanted so he can commit a robbery, or is wanted because he has committed a robbery. The later sense is the correct one. So too in this passage, the word "for" signifies an action in the past. Otherwise, it would violate the entire tenor of the NT teaching on salvation by grace and not by works.[30]

There are other passages that speak of "baptism" in a spiritual sense. Jesus speaks of his crucifixion as a "baptism" (Luke 12:5, Mark 10:38). 1 Peter 3:20-21 says that there is a

---

[30] (2001). In *Greek Dictionary* (electronic ed., p. 2). Ephesians Four Group.

baptism that "saves" us, but the context indicates that it does not refer to the ceremony of the sacrament, but to a spiritual baptism. He says in verse 21 that it symbolizes "...not the removal of dirt from the body but the pledge of a good conscience toward God," then continues, "It saves you by the resurrection of Jesus Christ."

Mark 16:16 says, "Whoever believes and is baptized will be saved". But it's important to note that he continues, "...but whoever does not believe will be condemned." The essential thing is to believe.

Practical Consequences

What are the practical consequences of the doctrine of salvation? No matter what church you belong to, or what your background is, I would like to make the following pastoral suggestions:

1. The most important question is, what are you trusting for your salvation? Or in whom are you trusting? Are you trusting your own efforts and good works? Are you trusting the fact that you have not committed any serious sins? Are you trusting the fact that you have been baptized or that you belong to the right church? If it is anything or anyone *besides* Christ, or *in addition to* Christ, that is *not* saving faith! The Bible teaches that our righteousness comes from God and it is by grace through faith.

Romans 1:17
For in the gospel a righteousness from God is revealed, a righteousness that is by faith *from first to last,* just as it is written: "The righteous will live by faith."

Ephesians 2:8-9

For it is by grace you have been saved, through faith -- and this *not from yourselves*, it is the gift of God -- *not by works,* so that no one can boast.

2. Secondly, if you are trusting Christ alone for your salvation, I want to encourage you to have *assurance of eternal life*. You can claim the promises of salvation by faith. Since eternal life is a gift, received by faith, we can know that we already have it. That *is not arrogance*, because your trust is *in the Lord*, not in your own *merits*. You no longer have to ask yourself, "Have I done enough? How good do I need to be?" The moment you believe in Jesus, you already have eternal life. Note the certainty in the following texts:

John 3:18

Whoever believes in him is not condemned, but whoever does not believe stands condemned already because he has not believed in the name of God's one and only Son.

John 5:24

I tell you the truth, whoever hears my word and believes him who sent me has eternal life and will not be condemned; *he has crossed over from death to life.*

1 John 5:12-13

He who has the Son has life; he who does not have the Son of God does not have life. I write these things to you who believe in the name of the Son of God *so that you may know that you have eternal life.*

Romans 8:38-39
    For I am convinced that neither death nor life, neither angels nor demons, neither the present nor the future, nor any powers, neither height nor depth, nor anything else in all creation, will be able to separate us from the love of God that is in Christ Jesus our Lord.

How comforting it is to rely on these promises! Remember the thief on the cross beside Jesus? What good works did he have time to do from the cross? Was he baptized? Did he become a member of the church? Did he help the poor? No! But what did Jesus tell him?

Luke 23:42-43
    Then he said, "Jesus, remember me when you come into your kingdom." Jesus answered him, "I tell you the truth, *today you will be with me in paradise.*"

3. Thirdly, if you understand that salvation is a gift, the motivation to live a good life should change. You don't need to gain "points" with God. You are now free to serve God and others simply out of gratitude, not out of fear or from a desire to gain something from God, but out of love.
    If you are a father or a mother, what do you want from your children? Brute obedience to avoid punishment? Insincere submission to get a reward? No! You want heartfelt, loving cooperation. Otherwise, it would be selfish, possibly manipulation. It's the same with God. He wants our obedience to be born out of love, not motivated by a fear of punishment or a desire for rewards.
    Continuing with the same analogy, if children trust their parents, they *obey* them. Haven't you thought this many times? Let's say a young child asks if he can stay up until

midnight. His parents know that he needs sleep, that he needs to get up early the next day, so they tell him no. Then the child argues and insists that he's not sleepy, that he'll be fine the next day, and refuses to go to bed. The parents think, "If he only trusted us, that we know what we're talking about, then he wouldn't argue with us!" It's the same with God. If we trust him, we submit to him. Our faith leads to genuine obedience that comes from the heart.

4. Fourthly, the sanctification that results from true faith is from the inside out, not patched on outwardly. It is produced by the Holy Spirit, not by human effort. This makes it lasting and effective.

We often try to make ourselves righteous. I know I grew up trying hard to be good, trying to keep all the rules. We know how we are expected to behave, so we force ourselves to do it. But in our hearts, the desire is not there. It may take a long time to discover this. It may require a tragedy or some difficult situation that exposes our superficiality, maybe a temptation that we weren't prepared to face. Then we see how weak we really are, that deep down inside we haven't really changed much by our own efforts. There's hostility, envy, resentment, selfishness, pride in our heart.

Then we can see ourselves in a mirror and identify with the Pharisees. Finally, when we give our hearts to the Lord and let him take over, he will do his own deep cleaning. He reaches down into our hearts and produces genuine fruit, rooted in love.

Questions for Review and Discussion
1. What is the difficulty in the interpretation of James 2?
2. What is the explanation given in this chapter of James 2?
3. What are the key definitions of the Greek word δικαιοω (dikaióo)? In what sense does Paul normally use the word in

Romans? In which of these senses does James use the term in chapter 2?

4. What is the difficulty of interpretation of Matthew 25?

5. What explanation is given in this chapter?

6. Describe the "divine illustration" in John 15 and explain how it helps understand the relation between faith and good works.

7. Explain the analogy of the orange trees and apple trees.

8. Explain the illustration of the light bulb.

9. How does the concept of the covenant help us understand what saving faith really is?

10. Explain the author's interpretation of Acts 2:38.

11. Describe the practical consequences a biblical view of salvation, according to the author.

4. The Bible Alone

Seeing, then, that we were too weak by unaided reason to find out the truth, and for this cause needed the authority of the holy writings, I had now begun to believe that Thou wouldest by no means have given such excellency of authority to those Scriptures throughout all lands, had it not been Thy will thereby to be believed in, and thereby sought.

(Augustine)[31]

I remember sitting in Sunday School with my parents when I was a young boy, listening to the teacher read from a magazine we called the *Quarterly*. It had a Bible passage and a few pages of explanation for each week of the three months. I knew the Bible was the holy inspired Word of God, and for a long time, I thought the explanatory section was also inspired. Nobody ever questioned the teachings of those *Quarterlies*. When I was in seminary, and during my first years in the ministry, I encountered people who almost seemed to consider the *Westminster Confession of Faith* inspired. However, if you asked my Sunday School teacher, my fellow seminary students, or my pastor friends, they would all agree that these documents are not inspired. Only the Bible is the inspired Word of God. The Bible alone is our authoritative source of truth. That's the traditional Protestant view.

The official Catholic position is that, not only is the Bible our authoritative source, but also *Tradition*. Thankfully, we

---

[31] Saint Augustine, *Confessions*, in *Basic Writings of Saint Augustine*, ed. Whitney J. Oates, vol. 1 (Grand Rapids, Michigan: Baker Book House, 1992), p. 78.

share a common trust in the Bible as the infallible Word of God, our divine authoritative revelation. Nevertheless, we are not in agreement about accepting *Tradition* as having the same authority as the Bible.

In one sense, "Faith Alone" is the most important issue, since it relates to our salvation. But "The Bible Alone" is also important, since many other doctrinal discussions depend on this one.

The Catholic View

What is *Tradition*? Here we are not using the word in the ordinary way of referring to customs; we are using it to refer to inspired teachings. Catholics believe that other teachings were handed down from Jesus and the apostles, truths that were not included in the Bible, but were passed down orally from generation to generation, being preserved by divine guidance among the authorities of the Church. They also believe that God has granted the authority to the Catholic Magisterium (the bishops and the pope) to give the correct interpretation of Scripture. Nobody else has that authority.

This doctrine was clearly expressed by the *Council of Trent*, probably to protect themselves from the teachings of the Reformation. It speaks of the "unwritten traditions" which were received from Christ and the apostles, "transmitted as it were from hand to hand," and "preserved in the Catholic Church by a continuous succession."[32]

The *Second Vatican Council* (1962-1965) declares that the apostles "left bishops as their successors, handing over to

---

[32] The Council of Trent, "Concerning the Canonical Scriptures," First Decree, Celebrated on the eighth day of the month of April, in the year 1546. <http://www.thecounciloftrent.com/ch4.htm>

them the authority to teach in their own place" and that the apostles' preaching is preserved "by an unending succession of preachers until the end of time...."[33]

The *Catechism* clarifies that Tradition has the same level of authority as Scripture.

> 82 As a result the Church, to whom the transmission and interpretation of Revelation is entrusted, "does not derive her certainty about all revealed truths from the holy Scriptures alone. *Both Scripture and Tradition must be accepted and honored with equal sentiments of devotion and reverence.*"

It also states that only the bishops and the pope can give the "authentic" interpretation of Scripture and Tradition:

> 85 "The task of giving an *authentic interpretation* of the Word of God, whether in its written form or in the form of *Tradition*, has been entrusted to the *living teaching office of the Church alone*. Its authority in this matter is exercised in the name of Jesus Christ." This means that *the task of interpretation has been entrusted to the bishops in communion with the successor of Peter, the Bishop of Rome.*

The position is clear. Both Scripture and Tradition are inspired and preserved by the Holy Spirit. Both are to be received and honored "with equal sentiments of devotion and reverence."

---

[33] "Dogmatic Constitution on Divine Revelation, *Dei Verbum*, Solemnly promulgated by His Holiness Pope Paul VI on November 18, 1965." Sections 7 y 8. <https://www.vatican.va/archive/hist_councils/ii_vatican_council/documents/vat-ii_const_19651118_dei-verbum_en.html> Read on Sept. 20, 2024.

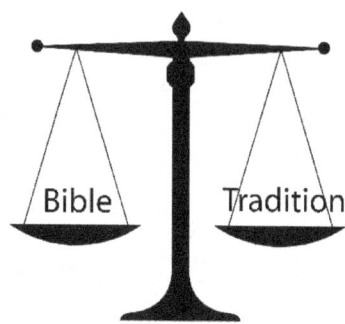

What Does Tradition Include?

Just what teachings are considered infallible *Tradition*? There is not complete agreement on the subject, but as I understand it, at least it includes the *ex cathedra* declarations of popes, as well as the statements in the creeds of ecumenical (or "general") councils.

Ex Cathedra Declarations

When the pope speaks *ex cathedra,* God's people should accept his declarations as divine revelation, along with the Bible. How do they know when the pope is speaking *ex cathedra*? Apparently, the pope himself can determine this. In 1993, Pope John Paul II explained that it must be "only in a doctrinal field limited to the truths of faith and morals and those closely connected with them" and that the pope must "clearly express his intention to define a certain truth and to demand the definitive adherence to it by all Christians."[34]

The *First Vatican Council* (1869-1870) declared that in these occasions, the pope possesses "infallibility...for defining

---

[34] Vatican News, "Primacy and infallibility: 150 years after Vatican I", July 17, 2020. <https://www.vaticannews.va/en/pope/news/2020-07/primacy-and-infallibility-150-years-after-vatican-i.html>

doctrine regarding faith or morals" and that these statements were "irreformable of themselves." [35]

Ex cathedra declarations don't happen very often. Two seemingly undisputed examples are the declaration of Pope Pius IX in 1854 regarding the immaculate conception of Mary (born without inheriting original sin) and the declaration by Pope Pius XII in 1950 regarding her bodily assumption into heaven without dying.

Creeds

The Catholic Church recognizes 21 councils as "ecumenical" and therefore infallible, beginning with the *First Council of Nicea* (325 AD), the *First Council of Constantinople* (381), and the *Council of Ephesus* (431), then continuing until the *Council of Trent* (1545-1563), the *First Vatican Council* (1868-1870) and the *Second Vatican Council* (1962-1965).[36]

The *Second Vatican Council* declares the infallibility of the bishops whenever they agree among themselves and with the pope, and when they are "authentically teaching on faith and morals." It is especially clear in an ecumenical council.[37]

The *Catechism* summarizes this:

---

[35] First Vatican Council, *Pastor Aeternus*, fourth session.
<https://www.catholicplanet.org/councils/20-Pastor-Aeternus.htm>
[36] Paul Senz, "The Authority of Ecumenical Councils", Catholic Answers
<https://www.catholic.com/magazine/print-edition/the-authority-of-ecumenical-councils>
[37] Dogmatic Constitution on the Church, Lumen Gentium, Solemnly Promulgated by His Holiness people Paul VI, on November 21, 1964, section 25.
<https://www.vatican.va/archive/hist_councils/ii_vatican_council/documents/vat-ii_const_19641121_lumen-gentium_en.html>

891 ...The infallibility promised to the Church is also present in the body of bishops when, together with Peter's successor, they exercise the supreme Magisterium, above all in an Ecumenical Council. When the Church through its supreme Magisterium proposes a doctrine "for belief as being divinely revealed," and as the teaching of Christ, the definitions must be adhered to with the obedience of faith.

The Protestant View

What is the Protestant perspective? First, while we respect the pre-reformation ecumenical councils, and find their creeds helpful summaries of biblical doctrine, Protestants believe that the only authoritative revelation remaining for the universal Church is the Bible. The *Westminster Shorter Catechism*, in the answer to question #2 says:

> The Word of God, which is contained in the Scriptures of the Old and New Testaments, is the only rule to direct us how we may glorify and enjoy him.

We believe that only the *written Scripture* comes with the divine guarantee of inspiration and infallibility for us today. Furthermore, it claims to be sufficient for our teaching and spiritual formation.

2 Timothy 3:16-17

All Scripture is God-breathed and is useful for teaching, rebuking, correcting and training in righteousness, *so that the man of God may be thoroughly equipped for every good work.*

Secondly, we believe that some Catholic doctrines that come from their Tradition are in direct contradiction with biblical teachings. After all, the *Council of Trent* was a reaction to the teachings of the Reformation. Some of the key doctrines regarding salvation that we discussed in previous chapters, such as justification by faith alone, were pronounced anathema by that council.

Thirdly, Protestants don't agree with the Catholic view of apostolic succession which includes the claim to infallibility and requires submission to their authority. Most Protestants agree that there was a special office of foundational apostles (Ephesians 2:19-20) who were inspired to write or to inform other writers of New Testament documents, and that this office ended with those who had been with Jesus (Acts 1:21-26) and with the composition of the New Testament.

Finally, isn't it questionable for church authorities to establish themselves as the only ones who can give the correct interpretation of Scripture and to declare themselves infallible? It's offensive to Christians outside their church, and it leaves no room for disagreement or dialogue.

Notice that we have seen again the same guiding principle that reinforces and maintains the Catholic Church: *submission to their authority.* Their doctrine of salvation requires their members to depend on them for redeeming grace, and their doctrine of Tradition requires them to depend on them as the source of true doctrine and for the correct interpretation of Scripture.

With this axiom, no other doctrine can be challenged, because it is not our place. If we disagree with the higher authorities, we are *ipso facto* wrong, with no right to question them! But listen to what Luke says about the Bereans:

Acts 17:11

Now the Bereans were of more noble character than the Thessalonians, for they received the message with great eagerness and examined the Scriptures every day to see if what Paul said was true.

It was "noble" of them to study the Scriptures, even to examine the teaching of the apostle Paul! Surely it would be proper to examine the teachings of the church authorities of our day!

Freedom of Conscience

The *Westminster Confession of Faith* was written in England during the Reformation, when they were struggling with the regulations and teachings of the Roman Catholic Church. Desiring to maintain their freedom of conscience, the reformers drafted the following statement:

God alone is Lord of the conscience, and hath left it free from the doctrines and commandments of men, which are, in anything, contrary to his Word; or beside it, in matters of faith, or worship. (Chapter 20, paragraph 2)

Note the distinction between the doctrines and commandments "contrary" to the Word of God and the doctrines and commandments "beside it." First, if we are told to do something or believe something "contrary" to the Word of God, we are free to *disobey* or *not believe*. For example, when the authorities forbade the apostles to teach in the name of Jesus (Acts 4: 18-20), the apostles insisted that they had to obey God above the civil authorities. For Protestants, the teaching of Mary's immaculate conception is "contrary" to the biblical teaching that all people are sinners (Romans 3:10-23), and therefore we should not believe it.

Secondly, *in matters of faith or worship*, we are free to obey or disobey even if we are told to do something that is not "contrary" to the Word of God, but "beside it. The area of freedom is even larger in these cases. (Or we could say the area of *authority* is smaller.) For example, if a pastor teaches that Jesus ate fish every day as a child, we don't have to believe it. If the pastor tells the men they should wear a tie when they attend worship, we don't have to obey such a command, because it is "beside" the Word of God. You may choose to go along with this in order to cooperate and keep peace, but you are not obligated biblically. In the same way, when the pope declares that Mary ascended into heaven without dying, we don't have to believe it. For us, it's a teaching "beside" the Bible, because the Bible neither affirms it nor denies it.

Questions for Review and Discussion
1. What authority do Catholics give to Tradition? Why?
2. Mention reasons Protestants do not accept Tradition as authoritative.
3. Explain the Protestant concept of freedom of conscience.

5. Jesus Alone

One thing Jesus asks me is that I lean totally on Him. That I trust only in Him, absolutely. That I abandon myself to Him without reserve.

(Mother Teresa) [38]

In Santiago, Chile, there is a hill in the center of town called *Cerro San Cristobal*. It's the tallest hill in the whole city. At the top is a large statue of the Virgin Mary, visible from any part of the city. Then about one hundred feet down the side of the hill, about one fourth the size, and hardly visible from anywhere in the city except right there on top of the hill, is a statue of Jesus. This is typical in many Latin American countries, and it symbolizes the high place given to Mary in the daily spiritual life of many people.

My wife, Angelica, is from Chile, where she studied in a Catholic school. She remembers an incident in a cathedral when she was a small girl. While she was watching all the people praying on their knees before a statue of Mary, she looked off to the side and saw a small statue of Jesus with nobody there! She felt sorry for him since they had left him all alone and went over to pray to him!

Both Catholics and Protestants consider Jesus our divine Lord and Savior, who lived a perfect life, went to the cross to pay for our sins, rose again from the dead, and will return again. In that sense, we both consider Jesus our only mediator for our salvation. Their *Catechism* says, "Jesus

---

[38] Mother Teresa, *Amor: Un Fruto Siempre Maduro; Breves Reflexiones de la Madre Teresa para cada día*, [English: The Best Gift is Love] (Buenos Aires: Editorial Atlántida, 1987), p. 29 (translated from Spanish by the author).

Christ is true God and true man, in the unity of his divine person; for this reason he is the one and only mediator between God and men." (Section 480). We do not have major differences regarding Christology.

However, there is an important difference in the role they attribute to the Virgin Mary and to the saints as mediators in the daily life of the Christian. They pray to Mary, to the saints, and hold special liturgical services in honor of the Virgin. Those who drafted *Evangelicals and Catholics Together* put this difference on their list as the following: "*Remembrance* of Mary and the saints or *devotion* to Mary and the saints." [39] That is, Protestants "remember" Mary and the saints, while Catholics are "devoted" to them. Some point to the importance of the mother as the emotional center of the Latin American family as an explanation of Mary's place in Latin American Catholicism.

The Catholic View

What is the official position of the Catholic Church? The logic of the Catholic view of Mary is that, since Mary is the mother of Jesus, she is also the mother of his body, the Church. This means she *cooperates in the work of redemption* in several ways: First, she gave birth to Jesus. This makes her the "Mother of God." Secondly, she aided the beginning of the Church with her prayers. Thirdly, she was born free of original sin and "participated" in Jesus' resurrection when she was taken to heaven without dying. This makes her "Queen over all things." In the fourth place, she is "the Church's model of faith and charity." Finally, she continues to intercede from heaven to bring us the "gifts of eternal salvation." These concepts are revealed in the *Catechism*:

---

[39] Colson and Neuhaus, *Evangelicals and Catholics Together*, p. xxi.

963 "The Virgin Mary ... is acknowledged and honored as being truly the *Mother of God* and of the redeemer.... She is 'clearly the *mother of the members of Christ*' ... since she has by her charity joined in bringing about the birth of believers in the Church, who are members of its head."

966 "Finally the Immaculate Virgin, *preserved free from all stain of original sin*, when the course of her earthly life was finished, *was taken up body and soul into heavenly glory*, and exalted by the Lord as *Queen over all things*, so that she might be the more fully conformed to her Son, the Lord of lords and conqueror of sin and death." The Assumption of the Blessed Virgin is a singular *participation in her Son's Resurrection* and an anticipation of the resurrection of other Christians.

968 "In a wholly singular way she *cooperated by her obedience, faith, hope, and burning charity in the Savior's work of restoring supernatural life to souls*. For this reason she is a mother to us in the order of grace."

969 "...Taken up to heaven she did not lay aside this saving office but by her manifold intercession *continues to bring us the gifts of eternal salvation*.... Therefore the Blessed Virgin is invoked in the Church under the titles of Advocate, Helper, Benefactress, and Mediatrix."

Although some theologians proposed the doctrine of the immaculate conception earlier, it was not until the 19th century that it became official. Saint Thomas Aquinas himself had denied this doctrine. The doctrine of the Assumption of the Virgin was accepted by the Catholic Church in 1950.[40] [41]

Catholic theologians insist that they do not "worship" Mary or the saints. However, the Catholic Church does dedicate "liturgical feasts" to her.[42] Catholics also pray directly to Mary. She is thought to be more "accessible" than God himself. Often they consider themselves unworthy to approach God directly, but trust that Mary will intercede for them. They find comfort in the maternal figure. The *Ave Maria* is a key example of this:

> 2677 Hail Mary, full of grace, the Lord is with thee.
> Blessed art thou among women and blessed is the fruit of thy womb, Jesus.
> 2677 Holy Mary, Mother of God, pray for us sinners, now and at the time of our death.

In one of the most critical times in life, at the moment of death, they are to "surrender wholly to her care." The *Catechism* explains why: she leads them to Jesus. She is called the "Mother of Mercy" and "the All-Holy One."[43]

As for the saints, Catholics consider that they are "witnesses" that have gone ahead of us to heaven, and that we "can and should ask them to intercede for us and for the whole world."[44]

---

[40] Rodolfo Blank, *Teología y misión*, p.66-68.

[41] <The Witness of the Church Fathers With Regard to Catholic Distinctives :: (catholicfidelity.com)> (June 4, 2024)

[42] *Catechism*, 971.

[43] *Catechism*, 2677.

[44] *Catechism*, 2683.

The Protestant View

Protestants believe that there is only one mediator between God and man, Jesus Christ, including for prayer and help with the daily Christian life.

1 Timothy 2:5
> For there is one God and one mediator between God and men, the man Christ Jesus.

The *Westminster Confession of Faith* says:

> Religious worship is to be given to God, the Father, Son, and Holy Ghost; and to him alone; not to angels, saints, or any other creature: and since the fall, not without a Mediator; nor in the mediation of any other but of Christ alone. (chapter 21, section 2)

Protestants believe that, because of Christ, we can pray directly to God. We can ask other people to pray *for us*, but we don't pray *to* anybody but God. We are not worthy in ourselves, but we come to him cleansed by the blood of Jesus. Jesus himself taught us to pray directly to the Father, in his name:

Matthew 6:9
> This, then, is how you should pray: "Our Father in heaven, hallowed be your name,"...

John 16:26-27
> In that day you will ask in my name. I am not saying that I will ask the Father on your behalf. No, the Father himself loves you because you have loved me and have believed that I came from God.

When Christ died, the curtain in the temple was torn from top to bottom (Matthew 27:51), symbolizing the fact that his death reconciled us to God and gave us access to him.

Hebrews 10:19-22
Therefore, brothers, since we have confidence to enter the Most Holy Place by the blood of Jesus, by a new and living way opened for us through the curtain, that is, his body, and since we have a great priest over the house of God, let us draw near to God with a sincere heart in full assurance of faith, having our hearts sprinkled to cleanse us from a guilty conscience and having our bodies washed with pure water.

We hold Mary in high esteem. We consider her "blessed among women," with her unique privilege of giving birth to Jesus and rearing him. She was also an example of faith and submission. We also admire those great Christians throughout history that have been examples to us of living a life dedicated to Christ and his people. However, we do not pray to them or consider them intercessors on our behalf. We don't believe that they *cooperate* in our salvation. Neither do we lift them up to a level above the rest of God's people. All of us are sinners, deserving condemnation.

Romans 3:10-12
There is no one righteous, not even one; ...there is no one who does good, not even one.

Romans 3:22-23

...There is no difference, for all have sinned and fall short of the glory of God.

We believe that Mary herself would want us to give all the attention to Jesus. Furthermore, the teachings about her immaculate conception and her ascension are additions to the Scriptures, accepted by Catholics because of their view of *Tradition*.

The gospel of Matthew tells of an incident that suggests Mary's ministry became less significant after Jesus began his public ministry.

Matthew 12:46-50

While Jesus was still talking to the crowd, his mother and brothers stood outside, wanting to speak to him. Someone told him, "Your mother and brothers are standing outside, wanting to speak to you."

He replied to him, "Who is my mother, and who are my brothers?" Pointing to his disciples, he said, "Here are my mother and my brothers. For whoever does the will of my Father in heaven is my brother and sister and mother."

It's clear that Mary was one of the people outside. The term "mother" would not refer to anybody else. And Jesus says that his true *mother and brothers and sisters* are those who do his Father's will.

We shouldn't minimize her privileged place in the story of redemption. However, this passage shows that neither should we honor her so highly as to call her "The All-Holy One" or "Queen over all things."

Questions for Review and Discussion

1. In common religious practice, what place is frequently given to Mary among Catholics?

2. According to the Catholic view, in what ways does Mary cooperate in the work of redemption?

3. Why do Catholics often pray to Mary?

4. What is the Protestant view of mediators?

5. Why can we pray directly to God?

6. What does Matthew 12:46-50 teach us about the attitude we should have toward Mary?

6. The Sacraments and Penance

On December 7 and 8, 2023, more than one million people made a pilgrimage to the Virgin of Lo Vásquez, about 40 miles from Santiago, Chile. This is a yearly celebration of the *Festival of the Immaculate Conception*. Some of them walk all the way from Santiago to make a promise, give thanks, or present a petition to the Virgin. Others are fulfilling their acts of *penance*, one of the Catholic sacraments.[45]

We've already seen how important the sacraments are in the Roman Catholic understanding of salvation. Now let's review their perspective on the sacraments in general, then focus on penance in particular, comparing their view with the Protestant view.

The Sacraments in General

Catholics have seven sacraments:
    Baptism
    Confirmation
    The Eucharist
    Penance
    Anointing the sick
    Ordination of priests, and
    Marriage

---

[45] <Más de 1 millón de peregrinos llegaron al Santuario de Lo Vásquez para agradecer y saludar a La Madre en la Fiesta de la Inmaculada Concepción - OBISPADO DE VALPARAÍSO (obispadodevalparaiso.cl/)> (June 12, 2024)

Protestants have only two:
 Baptism
 The Lord's supper (the Eucharist)

While we don't consider them sacraments, Protestants also practice three of the ceremonies considered sacraments by the Catholics: We receive members into the church, which is similar to confirmation, we also ordain pastors, and we celebrate marriages as a public promise in the church. This leaves two sacraments that we do not have: anointing the sick, and penitence. Some Protestants anoint the sick, but the practice does not have the same meaning as the Catholic sacrament. Penitence is related to the Protestant concept of repentance, but it is different. We will focus on penitence in this chapter.

But first, why do we have only two sacraments? Protestants have two criteria for defining a sacrament: 1) It must have been instituted by the Lord Jesus Christ Himself to be practiced by all believers. 2) It must be a ceremony that uses visible symbols to teach spiritual truths.

We don't include marriage and ordination as sacraments because they are not commanded for all believers. As for becoming a member of the church, we believe it is a step of commitment which should be taken by all believers, but it was not explicitly commanded by Jesus as a sacrament. Furthermore, Jesus didn't command the use of any visible symbols to be used in weddings, in ordination services, or in services to receive new members.

However, whether we call these ceremonies *sacraments* is not really what concerns us. The important thing is what significance is attributed to them.

The greatest difference lies in the fact that the Catholic Church considers sacraments necessary for salvation. To them, they are a part of the process of collaborating with the grace of God and doing merits. Catholic doctrine leads their members to depend on them and on the Catholic institution that administers them, for their salvation.

We already talked about the meaning of baptism for Catholics, under the topic of salvation. For them, it is the initial ceremony that imparts the grace of the Holy Spirit, regenerates the soul, and obtains forgiveness of sins.

Catholics also give a meaning to the Eucharist which is different from the Protestant concept. They teach that the bread and wine are actually converted into the body and blood of Jesus Christ in the mouth of the believer during the ceremony. (This is called "transubstantiation.")[46]

Protestants believe that these elements are symbols of spiritual truths. The Bible contains many figures of speech and symbols. For example, Jesus is given many names such as *the lamb of God* (John 1:24), *living water* (John 4:14), *bread of life* (John 6:35), *the gate* (John 10:11), and *the vine* (John 15:1). We don't interpret these phrases literally. We believe Jesus is also speaking figuratively when he says, "This is my body," and "This is my blood."

We believe that Jesus is spiritually present when we celebrate the Lord's Supper, but not physically present. His resurrected body is at the right hand of God the Father in heaven, not in all places at once.

In summary, we believe that the sacraments are ceremonies that use visible and tangible symbols to communicate spiritual truths. We believe that the sacraments operate much the same way the Bible does. The Bible contains words, but they are special words, chosen specifically by God Himself. God uses them to communicate

---

[46] *Catechism of the Catholic Church*, sections 1376 and 1413.

the gospel. Nevertheless, the effect depends on the work of the Holy Spirit and not on the act itself of reading. In a similar way, the water of baptism and the bread and wine of the Lord's Supper are chosen especially by God to communicate the gospel in a visible and tangible way. But the fact that someone participates in them does not automatically bring a spiritual effect on him. The results depend on the work of the Holy Spirit.

Penance

Penance is one of the Catholic sacraments that deserves special attention. It's related to what Protestants call "repentance," but it's actually quite distinct. There are two important differences:

1. First, the Roman Catholic Church emphasizes the need to make a confession before a priest, while Protestants focus only on confessing our sins directly to God in personal prayer.

While there are exceptions, normally a Catholic must go to confession for mortal sins (a more serious sin, especially related to breaking the Ten Commandments). For venial sins, it's not necessary, but it is recommended.[47]

> 1456 Confession to a priest is an essential part of the sacrament of Penance: "All *mortal sins* of which penitents after a diligent self-examination are conscious *must be recounted by them in confession,...*"

---

[47]<Do I Have to Go to Confession? | Catholic Answers Q&A> (June 5, 2024)
<*What to do if You Can't Go to Confession - The Bournemouth Oratory*> (June 5, 2024)

1458 Without being strictly necessary, confession of everyday faults (*venial sins*) is nevertheless strongly recommended by the Church...

While they recognize that only God can forgive sins, they believe that God has delegated authority to the bishops and priests to forgive sins in his name. They are mediators of God's grace.

1441 *Only God forgives sins*. Since he is the Son of God, Jesus says of himself, "The Son of man has authority on earth to forgive sins" and exercises this divine power: "Your sins are forgiven." Further, *by virtue of his divine authority he gives this power to men to exercise in his name.*

The *Catechism* says that the priests have the "power to forgive *all* sins."

1461 Since Christ entrusted to his apostles the ministry of reconciliation, *bishops* who are their successors, and *priests*, the bishops' collaborators, continue to exercise this ministry. Indeed bishops and priests, by virtue of the sacrament of Holy Orders, *have the power to forgive all sins* "in the name of the Father, and of the Son, and of the Holy Spirit."

In the formula for absolution, the priest says, "*I* absolve you from your sins." This is done in the name of God, but frankly I think this must be confusing to a person who goes to confession. It must seem like it is the priest who is deciding whether the person is forgiven or not.[48]

> 1449 ...*through the ministry of the Church* may God give you pardon and peace, *and I absolve you from your sins* in the name of the Father, and of the Son and of the Holy Spirit.

They base their doctrine on passages such as John 20:23 and Matthew 18:18

John 20:23
   If you forgive anyone his sins, they are forgiven; if you do not forgive them, they are not forgiven.

Matthew 18:18
   I tell you the truth, whatever you bind on earth will be bound in heaven, and whatever you loose on earth will be loosed in heaven.

Protestants, on the other hand, emphasize the fact that we can go directly to God to ask for pardon. The illustration of the difference between a scuba diver and a deep-sea diver applies again to this sacrament. In the Catholic view, the priests have been given the oxygen tanks to administer forgiveness. In the Protestant view, the diver receives the oxygen directly from God.

---

[48] See for example, <*How Can a Priest Forgive Sin? | Catholic Answers Magazine*> (June 5, 2024)

1 John 1:9

If we confess our sins, he is faithful and just and will forgive us our sins and purify us from all unrighteousness.

How do Protestants interpret passages like John 20:23 and Matthew 18:18? Some see these passages as a reference to the exercise of church discipline.[49] Protestant church leaders, pastors and elders, have the authority to exercise spiritual ecclesiastical discipline. This means that when a church member falls into sin, they call upon him to repent and do all they can to bring him back to Christ. But if the person continues in sin, rejecting their help, they may discipline him in various ways, maybe forbidding the person to take part in the Lord's Supper. In this case, they are "withholding forgiveness" or "binding" the person. However, this is not a declaration that God has not forgiven them. We don't know that. It refers only to their relation to the visible church. If the person repents, the church leaders have the authority to *restore him to fellowship*. In this case, they are "forgiving" them or "loosing" the person. (Matthew 18:15-20.) Again, this is not a declaration that God has forgiven the person. They can't know that for sure.

Others see the "forgiving" (or "liberating from sin") in these passages as a *proclamation of the gospel*, a *declaration that God forgives*.[50] This promise becomes a reality for those who truly repent and believe. This could be through personal

---

[49] Jamieson, R., Fausset, A. R., & Brown, D. (1997). *Commentary Critical and Explanatory on the Whole Bible* (Vol. 2, p. 169). Logos Research Systems, Inc.
[50] Hendriksen, W. (1981). *Comentario al Nuevo Testamento: El Evangelio según San Juan* (p. 737). Libros Desafío. William Hendriksen, *The Gospel According to John,* vol. 2 (Grand Rapids: Baker, 1983).

evangelism, the *preaching of the gospel in a sermon*,[51] or as an element of the worship service. Many Protestant worship services include a time of confession, either in the form of private prayer or in the form of reading together a prepared statement, followed by an assurance of pardon. The difference is that the person leading the service doesn't say, "I absolve you from your sins." Instead, he tells the congregation that *God* forgives those who are trusting Christ. Normally, in this case it comes in the form of a Scripture reading that includes the promise of forgiveness.

The concern of Protestants is not with Catholics confessing their sins to a priest. The issue is how people seek pardon for sins and assurance of that pardon. Catholics depend on the Church, the clergy, and the sacraments. Protestants claim the promise of forgiveness directly from *God himself.*

2. The second difference between Catholic penance and Protestant repentance is that the priest instructs the confessor to perform certain acts of penance to "repair the damage." If he has done harm to someone, he should make amends. In the same way, he should make amends for the damage done to his relationship with God and be restored to him. For example, if we rob someone, we need to give back what we stole and we should also make amends for the damage done to our relationship with God. That is why the priest gives the penitent person religious exercises, especially prayers, works of mercy, or some kind of sacrifice.

Protestants agree that sometimes we should repair the damage we have done, ask forgiveness from those we have

---

[51] Guthrie, D. (1994). *John.* In D. A. Carson, R. T. France, J. A. Motyer, & G. J. Wenham (Eds.), *New Bible commentary: 21st century edition* (4th ed., p. 1063). Inter-Varsity Press.

offended, and change our behavior. However, the problem is that Catholics speak of "expiating" their sin, of "making satisfaction" for it. This terminology seems to communicate the idea that he is not fully forgiven until he has done his "penance" activity.

> 1459 Many sins wrong our neighbor. One must do what is possible in order to *repair the harm* (e.g., return stolen goods, restore the reputation of someone slandered, pay compensation for injuries). But sin also injures and weakens the sinner himself, as well as his *relationship with God and neighbor*. Absolution takes away sin, but it does not remedy all the disorders it has caused. Raised up from sin, the sinner must still recover his full health by doing something more to make amends for the sin: *he must "make satisfaction for" or "expiate" his sin.* This satisfaction is also called "penance."

> 1460 The *penance* the confessor imposes must take into account the penitent's personal situation and must seek his spiritual good. It must correspond as far as possible with the gravity and nature of the sins committed. *It can consist of prayer, an offering, works of mercy, service of neighbor, voluntary self-denial, sacrifices, and above all the patient acceptance of the cross we must bear.*

The concept of "penance" can be confusing. Since the relationship with God is not fully restored without acts of penance, the person must think his own actions have helped earn his forgiveness. On the other hand, a person can begin to think he has never done enough. This mentality often leads to participating in pilgrimages like the one in Chile mentioned previously. Martin Luther, when he was in the monastery before his conversion, fasted, slept in the cold without blankets, and demanded of himself long prayer vigils and Bible reading, punishing himself until he became a mere skeleton. He wrote, "If I had kept on any longer, I would have killed myself...."[52] Others may trust in their own suffering, thinking that God will reward them for it. It takes their eyes off Jesus who already suffered for our sins and offers free forgiveness.

For example, I knew an elderly gentleman who had a serious problem with his leg. The doctors had operated on him more than twenty times, and the results were never what they promised. He was living with severe pain in his leg and in his back. He walked with great difficulty, using a cane. He finally concluded that the doctors were making themselves rich at the expense of his suffering. It was a bitter realization. When he came to talk to me about his relationship with his wife, I took the opportunity to talk with him also about his relationship with God. I asked him if he thought he had eternal life and he said, "Yes, I do." When I asked him why, he broke down crying and answered, "Because I have tried to live a good life, and because I have suffered so much."

While it is true that our relationship with God is damaged by sin, God himself tells us what will restore that relationship: He tells us to confess our sin to him and he will "forgive us our sins and purify us of all unrighteousness." He doesn't ask us to do anything else. Of course, prayer, Bible Study, and acts of mercy are certainly means of spiritual growth. Furthermore, there may be a need to make amends for harm done to another person, such as paying them back for what was stolen. This is simply something that should be

---

[52] Ronald Bainton, *Here I Stand; a Life of Martin Luther* (Nashville, Tennessee: Abingdon Press, 1950), p. 45.

done for the sake of justice. But these acts are not substitutes for God's forgiving mercy. We can never "expiate" our sin. Jesus already did that!

Questions for Review and Discussion
1. What are the Protestant criteria for defining a "sacrament?"
2. What is the greatest difference between the Catholic and Protestant views of the sacraments?
3. What is the Catholic doctrine of "transubstantiation?"
4. What are the differences between the Catholic concept of penance and the Protestant view of repentance?

7. The Papacy and Church Government

I'll never forget the visit of Pope John Paul II to Chile. It was one of the biggest events I have ever seen. Multitudes lined the streets where he would pass by, all over Santiago. As he came near, people pushed and shoved, struggling to get a view of him, like they did for war heroes in Europe after World War II. I myself went to the Parque Forestal to observe the procession. The mob was so thick that my friend and I had to take turns riding "piggyback" to see him. I could sense how important the pope is for many Roman Catholics.

The Catholic View

The power of the roman papacy was established during the fifth century under Pope Leo I (440-461). One of the main causes was the fact that they had experienced so many doctrinal controversies during the first three centuries. They had debated the doctrine of the Trinity, the nature and person of Jesus, Pelagianism, and the biblical canon, for example. Who determined which doctrines were correct? Thus Rome was established as the ecclesiastical center, to assure unity of thought and to avoid heresy. Leo I argued that Peter was the gate-keeper of the Kingdom, the "rock" upon which the Church was built, and that the pope was his successor. He obtained an edict from emperor Valentinian III, which demanded obedience to the pope.[53]

---

[53] Kenneth Scott Latourette, *A History of Christianity* (New York: Harper and Row, 1953) pp. 185-187.

Pope Gregory VII (Hildebrand) established a more solid position of the pope in the eleventh century (1073-1085), giving him power over civil authorities. In this period, *Dicatus Papae* was published, a document probably written by Gregory himself, with 26 affirmations. It included the following: 1. Princes must kiss the feet of the pope, 2. The pope cannot be judged by anybody, 3. The Roman Catholic Church never has committed any error, and 4. The pope has authority to remove emperors from their thrones.[54]

The *Catechism* emphasizes the doctrine that the pope is the successor of Peter, he is head of the Church, and he is infallible when making an official proclamation of doctrine or morality. We saw this concept of infallibility previously when we studied their view of *Tradition*.

> 882 The Pope, Bishop of Rome and Peter's successor, "is the perpetual and visible source and foundation of the unity both of the bishops and of the whole company of the faithful." "For the Roman Pontiff, by reason of his office as Vicar of Christ, and *as pastor of the entire Church has full, supreme, and universal power over the whole Church, a power which he can always exercise unhindered.*"

> 890 ...Christ endowed the Church's shepherds with the charism of *infallibility* in matters of faith and morals. The exercise of this charism takes several forms.

> 891 "The Roman Pontiff, head of the college of bishops, enjoys this *infallibility* in virtue of his office,...

---

[54] Latourette, pp. 470-473.

The biblical passage cited to defend Peter as the first "pope" is Matthew 16:15-19, where Jesus tells Peter that he is the "rock," and that he will build his church upon the rock. He also tells him that he will give him the "keys to the kingdom."

Matthew 16:15-19
"But what about you?" he asked. "Who do you say I am?" Simon Peter answered, "You are the Christ, the Son of the living God." Jesus replied, "Blessed are you, Simon son of Jonah, for this was not revealed to you by man, but by my Father in heaven. And I tell you that you are Peter, and on this rock I will build my church, and the gates of Hades will not overcome it. I will give you the keys of the kingdom of heaven; whatever you bind on earth will be bound in heaven, and whatever you loose on earth will be loosed in heaven."

The Protestant View

Protestants don't recognize the pope as the head of the universal Church. We don't object to the fact that Catholics have established an office of maximum authority for their own church, but we disagree with the claim that he has exclusive superior authority over the whole universal Church. This implies that any church that doesn't recognize the pope is not really part of the universal Church.

1) First, we consider Peter and the other apostles a unique group of people that God chose to be the foundation of the church.

Ephesians 2:19-20
Consequently, you are no longer foreigners and aliens, but fellow citizens with God's people and members of God's household, built on the foundation of the apostles and prophets, with Christ Jesus himself as the chief cornerstone.

We believe that the leaders of the church after the time of the New Testament are *not* part of the foundation. There is only one foundation and it was already laid. The future leaders are stones built on top of it.

2) Second, let's take another look at Matthew 16:15-19.
Jesus is not talking about the structure of the Church as an institution here. In fact, Jesus never explained exactly what structure the church should have.
Then what did Jesus mean? When he refers to the "rock," he is making a play on words. He tells Simon that he is "Peter," and on this "rock" he will build his Church. The name "Peter" ("petros") is a masculine form of the word "petra," the more commonly used word for "rock." Obviously, Jesus is giving Peter a special ministry.
What is that ministry? Peter had just confessed his faith in Christ, and in a sense became the first "member" of the New Testament Church. Peter is also the first *leader* of the New Testament Church, the first human instrument used to establish it. Peter preached the first sermon in Jerusalem and three thousand were converted (Acts 2). He apparently directed the first church councils (Acts 15) and gave his approval to include the Gentiles in the Church.
The problem with the Catholic interpretation of Matthew 16 is *not* that Peter be considered the "rock" upon which Jesus builds his church. *The problem is in establishing a*

perpetual hierarchy, a successive papacy, with dogmatic authority. There is only one rock and one foundation. As the "rock" and as an apostle, Peter is part of that initial "foundation." But this doesn't suggest a continual succession of leaders. Jesus doesn't say Peter is the first of many "rocks."

Now let's look at the "keys to the kingdom." What are they? The keys are for "binding" and "loosing."

> Matthew 16:19
> I will give you the keys of the kingdom of heaven; whatever you bind on earth will be bound in heaven, and whatever you loose on earth will be loosed in heaven.

Notice the parallel concept in Matthew 18:18. Here Jesus is not speaking to Peter, but to a larger group of disciples. Peter is not the only one who received the "keys."

> Matthew 18:18
> I tell you the truth, whatever you bind on earth will be bound in heaven, and whatever you loose on earth will be loosed in heaven.

In what sense to the disciples bind and loose? In a previous chapter, we mentioned several possible meanings: a) The church leaders can restore those who have strayed from the right path. This is the context of Matthew 18 (See Matthew 18:15-17.) b) They can pray for people. This is suggested in Matthew 18:20. ("For where two or three come together in my name, there am I with them.") c) They can proclaim the gospel with others, promising forgiveness and freedom from the power of sin. We read throughout the book of Acts how Peter and the apostles did this as the churches were established throughout the Mediterranean area. These are three ways to use the "keys to the kingdom," because they free people from sin and its consequences.

3) Finally, even if we accepted the concept of apostolic succession, how do we know who succeeds Peter? How do we know it isn't the Ecumenical Patriarch of the Eastern Orthodox Church or the pope of the Coptic Orthodox Church, for example? How do we know the ministers who wrote the *Westminster Confession of Faith* did not inherit the authority to give the infallible interpretation of Scripture?

A major cause of the division between the Western Church and the Eastern Church in 1054 was the power struggle between Rome and Constantinople. The culmination of this conflict was that both the pope in Rome and the Patriarch of Constantinople mutually excommunicated each other.[55] How do we know which side has the legitimate successor to Peter?

Church Government

We can't speak of *the* Protestant system of church government, because there are different forms within Protestantism. We don't consider church structure as something that has been mandated in the Bible. Nevertheless, historically there is a difference between Protestant and Catholic ecclesiastical structure in most denominations. (The Anglicans are an exception; they have a hierarchy similar to the Catholics.) Among Protestants, the church members normally participate in the selection of the pastor and other leaders, probably voting at some point in

---

[55] "Schism of 1054", <https://www.britannica.com/event/Schism-of-1054> Feb. 8, 2018.

the process. The members also usually participate in important decisions like the approval of the budget.

In the Catholic system, the members of the local church do not decide who will be their priest or who will be their leaders. On the contrary, the superior authorities assign them.

The positive aspect of the Catholic system is that it reflects the fact that the ultimate authority over the Church comes from above, from Christ. Another positive factor is that they manifest the unity of the Church. However, the problem with the Catholic system is that is does not reflect the fact that the lay believers are also brothers, that they are equals before God, and that they have the same Holy Spirit.

Protestants don't want to lose sight of the fact that Jesus is head of the Church, and that he has given authority to the leaders. Nevertheless, each member is considered equal in Christ and is given voice and vote in congregational meetings. In the Protestant system, the authority "from above" is seen in the leadership, but there is also authority "from below" seen in the voting participation of the members.

What kind of structure did the church have in New Testament times? In the first place, we observe the participation of "lay people" in important decisions, such as the election of deacons.

Acts 6:2-6
... So the Twelve gathered *all the disciples* together and said, "It would not be right for us to neglect the ministry of the word of God in order to wait on tables. Brothers, choose seven men from among you who are known to be full of the Spirit and wisdom. We will turn this responsibility over to them and will give our

attention to prayer and the ministry of the word." This proposal pleased *the whole group*. They chose Stephen, a man full of faith and of the Holy Spirit; also Philip, Procorus, Nicanor, Timon, Parmenas, and Nicolas from Antioch, a convert to Judaism. They *presented these men to the apostles*, who prayed and laid their hands on them.

Notice that the apostles gathered the "all the disciples" and asked them to pick out seven good men to serve tables. Apparently the "whole group" chose the deacons, but the apostles laid hands on them to officially name them. This reflects both the authority of the leaders and the voice of the members.

Secondly, there was a certain unity among the congregations. This unity is manifested in the first council of Jerusalem.

Acts 15:2

This brought Paul and Barnabas into sharp dispute and debate with them. So Paul and Barnabas were appointed, along with some other believers, to go up to Jerusalem to see the apostles and elders about this question.

Third, in the early church, there were apparently two offices: elders (or presbyters) and deacons. The deacons seemed to supervise the physical-material aspects of the church (Acts 6), and the elders supervised the more pastoral matters. The elders were also called "bishops" or "overseers." The terms seem to be synonymous in Titus 1.

Titus 1:5,7
(5) The reason I left you in Crete was that you might straighten out what was left unfinished and appoint *elders* (or "presbyters", in Greek: πρεσβύτερος, prebúteros) in every town, as I directed you.
(7)...Since an *overseer* (or "bishop" in KJV and ASV, in Greek: ἐπίσκοπος, epíscopos) is entrusted with God's work, he must be blameless.

Some of the presbyters dedicated more time to the pastoral work and deserved a salary. But apparently there was no distinction made in authority; all the elders were considered equal.

1 Timothy 5:17-18
The elders who direct the affairs of the church well are worthy of double honor, especially those whose work is preaching and teaching. For the Scripture says, "Do not muzzle the ox while it is treading out the grain," and "The worker deserves his wages."

The conclusions that we draw from the texts about the early church structure are:

1) The members participated in the selection of leaders.
2) Once chosen, the leaders supervised over the local church.
3) The leaders of the local church also took problems to a higher council.
4) There was a manifestation of unity among the churches.
5) There were two offices: elders (presbyters) and deacons.
6) The term "bishop" was also used interchangeably with "elder."

Questions for Review and Discussion

1. What historical problem influenced the development of the papacy?

2. What biblical passage do Catholics use to support the papacy?

3. How do Protestants interpret the fact that Peter is called the "rock?"

4. How do Protestants interpret the concept of the "keys" to the kingdom?

5. What is one of the main differences between the Catholic and Protestant systems of church government in general?

6. Where do we see in the New Testament that the members of the congregation participated in important decisions?

7. Name six conclusions we can draw about the organization of the New Testament churches.

Conclusion

I hope that I have spoken with respect for Catholics. I don't want to hide my disagreements with their positions on the issues covered in this book, especially the three "solos," or three "alones": 1) faith alone, 2) the Bible alone, and 3) Jesus alone. But I want to insist again that I have great respect for them, their institution, and their theologians. I am also aware of how the Lord is working among them and through them. I want to acknowledge especially how thankful I am for all the ways that they help needy people around the world. And I repeat that I have been dealing, as well as I can discern, with the official doctrines of the Roman Catholic Church and traditional Protestant churches. I realize that not all people hold the official position of their churches.

The study of Catholic doctrine challenges me to reflect especially in the area of the church as a body. We Protestants tend to be very individualistic in our relationship with the Lord, neglecting how God treats his children as a people. We have a challenge: to study more about the corporal aspect of faith, give greater importance to the people of God as a community, and express in our way of life the unity of the church. The concept of the covenant is key for us in this study, a theme very dear to Protestants, but a concept that needs to be applied better.

I would like to end by challenging the reader, whether Catholic or Protestant, to consider what the implications of these doctrines are in his or her own life. Think especially of salvation by faith alone. Do you really trust Jesus for your salvation, or are you relying also on something else to merit eternal life?

You may feel like a mountain climber hanging on to a rock, high above the canyon. You want to climb to the top, but you are exhausted. You may be afraid to move. You may think that things such as baptism, the sacraments, your own righteousness, or your own suffering, will help save you, so you refuse to let go of them. You have a heavy bag full of them. But as long as you hang on to them, you will not make it to the top. They will just weigh you down. And as long as you cling to the side of the cliff, you will not move upward. I want to assure you that Jesus is right there, waiting to take your hand. You must let go of all other hopes, take His hand, and he will *pull* you up to safety.

Why did Jesus die on the cross? What did he accomplish there? Just a partial contribution to your salvation? No! He purchased your *complete* salvation! All you need to do is trust him!

Remember the questions from *Evangelism Explosion?*:

If you were to die today, do you think you would go to heaven?

If you were to die and go before God, and he asked you why you think you could have eternal life, what would you answer?

How would you answer these questions now?

If you are still imagining a "balancing scales" view of salvation, please change that image in your mind. We are all sinners and you can never earn your own eternal life! You can only throw yourself on God's mercy! You can be saved only because Jesus died for you! Take your sins and pretended merits to the foot of the cross and leave them there!

Psalm 103:11-13
For as high as the heavens are above the earth, so great is his love for those who fear him; as far as the east is from the west, so far has he removed our transgressions from us. As a father has compassion on his children, so the Lord has compassion on those who fear him;

The Three "Alones"		
Doctrine	**Protestant View**	**Roman Catholic View**
1. Salvation	**By faith alone** (Works are evidence and fruit of true faith.)	By baptism + other sacraments + faith + merits
2. Authority	**The Bible alone**	The Bible + Tradition
3. Mediators	**Jesus alone**	Jesus + The Virgin Mary + the saints

Bibliography

Augustine. *Confessions.* London: Penguin Books, 1973.

Berkhof, Louis. *The History of Christian Doctrines.* Grand Rapids, Michigan: Baker Book House, 1975.

Blank, Rodolfo, *Teología y misión en América Latina.* St. Louis, Missouri: Concordia, 1996.

Catechism of the Catholic Church. New York: Doubleday, 1995.

Colson, Charles, y Neuhaus, Richard John. *Evangelicals and Catholics Together; Toward a Common Mission.* Dallas, Texas: Word Publishing, 1995.

Documentos del Concilio Ecuménico Vaticano II. México: Ediciones Paulinas, 1983.

Documents of the Christian Church. ed. Henry Bettenson. London: Oxford University Press, 1963.

La Fe Católica; Textos Doctrinales del Magisterio de la Iglesia. ed. G. Dumeige. Barcelona: Editorial Estela, 1965.

Hägglund, Bengt. *History of Theology.* St. Louis, Missouri: Concordia Publishing House, 1966.

Kennedy, James. *Evangelism Explosion*. Chicago: Tyndale House
    Publishers, 1977.

Latourette, Kenneth Scott. *A History of Christianity*. New York:
    Harper and Row,1953.

Madre Teresa. *Amor: Un Fruto Siempre Maduro*; *Breves
    Reflexiones de la Madre Teresa para cada día*. Buenos Aires:
    Editorial Atlántida, 1987.

Tamaro, Susana . *Donde el Corazón te Lleve*. Santiago de Chile:
    Editorial Atlántida, 1995.

The Westminster Confession of Faith. Version published by the
    Committee for Christian Education and Publications of the
    Presbyterian Church in America, 1983, together with the
    Larger Catechism and the Shorter Catechism with Scripture
    Proofs.